An Unapologeti...
of the Powe...

The SUBSTANCE OF THINGS HOPED FOR

DENNIS D. SEMPEBWA, PH.D.

The SUBSTANCE OF THINGS HOPED FOR

An Unapologetic Exposition of the Power of Faith

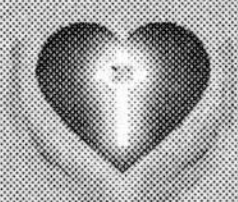

Hunter Heart Publishing
Colorado Springs, Colorado

The Substance of Things Hoped For

First Edition: October 2015
Second Edition: November 2015

To order products, or for any other correspondence:

Hunter Heart Publishing
4164 Austin Bluffs Parkway, Suite 214
Colorado Springs, Colorado 80918
www.hunterheartpublishing.com
Tel. (253) 906-2160 – Fax: (719) 368-6655
E-mail: publisher@hunterheartpublishing.com
Or reach us on the internet: www.hunterheartpublishing.com
"Offering God's Heart to a Dying World"

This book and all other Hunter Heart Publishing™ Eagle's Wings Press™ and Hunter Heart Kids™ books are available at Christian bookstores and distributors worldwide.

Chief Editor: Gord Dormer
Book cover design: Phil Coles Independent Design
Layout & logos: Exousia Marketing Group www.exousiamg.com
ISBN: 978-1-937741-66-2 Ebook ISBN: 978-1-937741-67-9
Printed in the United States of America.

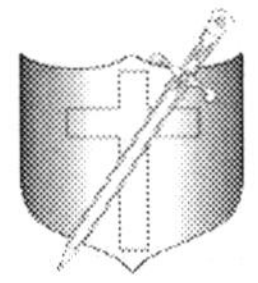

"NOW FAITH IS <u>THE SUBSTANCE</u> OF THINGS HOPED FOR, THE EVIDENCE OF THINGS NOT SEEN."

~HEBREWS 11:1~

ENDORSEMENTS

There are good books that encourage and challenge me to walk wild with my Jesus; books with a message that speaks straight to my heart. The Substance is one of them! This book will wake up a desire you didn't know you had inside you to give everything to Jesus. It will stir you up to walk with the Holy Spirit in great authority. Simple, childlike and radical.

Matthias Schinkelshoek
Founder, OpenHouse4Cities
Thun, Switzerland

"Believe the Gospel," "... if you have faith and do not doubt," "... if you have faith as small as a mustard seed". Throughout the Scriptures, God calls us to a life of faith. Dennis Sempebwa is a man of faith. He understands faith intellectually—he is steeped in Scripture. But more than that, he understands faith experientially. Growing up amid the horrors of war-torn Uganda during the reign of Idi Amin, Dennis was forced to rely on faith over and over again. Living like this builds and strengthens faith in the power of God. This faith has grown and deepened through years of global ministry. Now Dennis distills all he has learned about faith in this wonderful book. It is a book that should be read slowly. It is a book that shows us how to live faithfully, expectantly, and powerfully for God's glory.

Dr. John Van Wagoner
Chairman, Scripture Awakening
Hendersonville, NC, U.S.A.

My personal definition of faith is hearing God, believing all He says and living consequently. Well, Dr. Dennis Sempebwa, whom I am honored to have known for several years, is a man of vibrant and real faith. The insights found in this amazing book can't be attained just by research and study, but by pure revelation and experience. I strongly encourage those who want to know and experience real faith, to read this book.

Pastor Pietro Evangelista
Publisher, Evangelista Media (Formerly Destiny Image Europe)
Pescara, Italy

In this fast moving world, we find some of the most complex of problems. Mankind is crying out for a simple answer; one that is removed from gimmickry and needless shenanigans. Is there an answer? Can we really trust in an unseen God in this age? What my dear friend Dennis has done here is point us back to the simplicity of Jesus' teachings. This is simply told; demonstrated in a life lived out after the same simple principles.

Dr. Pete Odera
Founder, The Waterbrook
Nairobi, Kenya

The subject of faith is timeless. As a Spiritual Mother to Dr. Dennis for the past twenty years, I have witnessed the power of God and faith activated in his life. In his book, The Substance, Dr. Dennis uniquely identifies the different types of faith and the significance they have on us as believers. As Dr. Dennis expresses in this book, sometimes God will lead us right into a "savage storm." It's during this season in our lives that we must have reckless faith. Reckless faith helps us to step out of the boat of doubt and into the arms of a God who can, and will, do the miraculous in our lives! As you digest the words of this book, you will be healed and transformed—spirit, soul, and body! Your faith will be full and you will be able to believe God for ANYTHING!

Dr. Ruth Peterson
Senior Pastor, The Anointed Ones Church of Deliverance International
Ayden, NC, U.S.A.

The Substance—an interesting title selection by my brother. Dr. Dennis suggests that faith is not a nothing, but very much a living, breathing, tangible something. In his unique and engaging writing style, he weaves a colorful tapestry on the imagination, taking the reader on a journey from the shores of Galilee to the shores of Lake Victoria, and back again. His is a life that should not have been … but God. I am a witness! God is no respecter of persons. He has done it before, and He will do it again. We only need a little substance. I deeply appreciate this work, and the heart from which it emanates.

Pastor Zerubabbel B. Mengistu
Senior Pastor, Beza International Church
Addis Ababa, Ethiopia

Dr. Sempebwa's book speaks to the very core of what God asks of us: to have the kind of faith that allows us to give ourselves to Him—heart, mind, soul, spirit, body, gifts, and talents. To give Him something to touch, and watch Him bless it and cause it to become more than enough!

Father Michael Pfleger
Pastor, Faith Community of St. Sabina
Chicago, IL, U.S.A.

I highly recommend this book to anyone who is concerned for the future. Dr. Sempebwa presents, in each chapter, a challenge to see that each of us can make a difference in this ever-changing world. Thank you Dr. Dennis, for reminding us that now more than ever—whatever we can offer can be multiplied in the nail-scarred Hands of Jesus!

Pastor Mary Alice Schroeder
Pastor, Good News Church
Riverside, CA, U.S.A.

Faith. It starts on such an elementary level, yet it grows and expands as far and wide as we are willing to take it. Faith has no boundaries, no limits. Faith must be a continual work in our lives. It can never lie dormant or stagnant. Faith must grow. In The Substance, Dr. Dennis lays out a wonderful journey to engage and grow our faith. The danger of a topic so familiar is the ease of overlooking the importance for continual growth. So many in the Christian world stop maturing their faith at the introductory level. Dennis' book releases the stories of true, expanding faith. The book is more than a challenge—it is a guide for growth. The journey is both entertaining and inspiring. Explore the book and let the book explore you. Your faith will never be the same.

Rev. Scott Holmes
District Superintendent, Assemblies of God
Alexandria, LA, U.S.A.

In a world filled with uncertainty and insecurity, developing scriptural-based faith is not an option but a necessity for believers everywhere. In The Substance, my friend Dr. Dennis Sempebwa expounds on this vital subject of faith in a unique and practical style, which challenges and inspires the reader to continue trusting in the Lord no matter the trials.

Pastor William Michael Nsubuga
Leader, Smyrna International Church
Gothenburg, Sweden

Every decade, a Christian literary work and resource stirs the gift of faith within me like a Holy Windstorm. This book will do the same in you. While most people build walls for a windstorm, Dr. Dennis' godly insight will inspire you to build windmills.

Dr. Phillip Myles
Lead Elder of Prayer, Christ Church of The Valley
San Dimas, CA, U.S.A.

I was gripped from the very first words of this book as the message of pure, simple, child-like faith resonated loudly within my heart; that faith without which we cannot please God. Thank you Father for this fresh manna from heaven and thank you Dr. Dennis for your obedience in putting pen to paper by writing *The Substance*. We only have to look around us to see that we are living in the last days; I really believe that The Substance is one of the key books apart from the Bible that every disciple of the Kingdom of God needs to read again and again before the return of our Lord Jesus!

Sergio Benjumea
Missionary, Heaven's Ambassadors to the Nations
Chester, U.K.

I have known Dr. Dennis Sempebwa for three to four years. I've sat under his teaching and participated in ministry with him here in America, as well as in Uganda and Kenya. He is a solid preacher of the Word of God. If I could think of one theme that epitomizes Dr. Dennis' life and ministry, it would be Faith! He walks in faith more than any man I know. I love to read books by those who are "doers" of the Word, not just those who merely "hear" or "proclaim" it. We do have great teachers in God's Kingdom, but I love to follow and learn from men of God who are doers of the Word. Dr. Dennis Sempebwa fulfills these criteria for me. The topics of this new book are pages from his life.

Dr. James Hanley
Pastor, Moriah Bible Church / Moriah Freedom Ministry
Orange, CA, U.S.A.

I met Dennis Sempebwa over lunch at a local hotel restaurant on the recommendation of a mutual friend. My experience of African ministries before that day had been mostly via Christian TV broadcasts. Dennis was a total contradiction to my perceived stereotype—he was quiet-spoken, humble and surprisingly honest and open. Later that week, I watched him minister to about twenty people in a friend's living room. He was patient, gentle and compassionate as he took time with each individual. He prophesied words of release and encouragement with remarkable accuracy and impact. Since then, Dennis has ministered to our small church on a number of occasions, each time with great effect. The greatest compliment I can pay Dennis is that He represents Jesus well, both in character and gifting. I count myself extremely privileged to have him as a friend and as such I unreservedly recommend his new book. This is not theological theory. Dennis has lived what he has written and calls us all to a greater encounter with Him who is the 'Substance' of faith.

Dr. Steven Dobbins
Senior Pastor, Bethel
Wirral, England

Wow! What an amazing compilation of God-inspired words to build our faith. This book challenges you to be certain you possess the Kingdom currency called Faith. I would encourage you to read these truths with an open mind and release your faith in your spheres of influence. May your faith be inspired to new places as you turn each page. Thank you for a right now word, Dr. Dennis.

Dr. Dexter Ball
Faithwalk Harvest Church
Carpentersville, IL, U.S.A.

It is an honor to speak about Pastor Dennis. I have been strongly affected by his humble and simple character, while also motivated by his full passion for the Lord. Both my life, and the lives of the members of my church in Sevilla, has been greatly blessed. We have received great blessings through his teachings, backed by the power of the Holy Spirit. I am convinced that through the pages of this book, the reader will be permeated by the spirit of faith and passion that surrounds the life of its author.

Pastor Daniel C. Romero
Pastor, Centro Cristiano Encuentro Con Jesus
Carmona, Spain

The Substance is very refreshing. It is a treasure of time-tested truths that liberate and empower believers to succeed in life. The life we know today is a reflection of the thoughts we embrace. In The Substance, Dr. Dennis shares the thoughts that have equipped him for success in his life-journey; now he openly shares them with the world.

Pastor Tafforest D. Brewer
Senior Pastor, House of Faith International Church
Bloomington, IL, U.S.A.

Dr. Dennis has been able to break down the subject of faith in a way most have never done. The Substance is for every student of faith—as every believer should be. As you study these sixteen dimensions of faith, let this be a witness to your spirit, soul, and body and allow the revelation to water every dry place. A must read!

Pastor Julian Kyula
Raising Kingdom Champions, Inc.
Nairobi, Kenya

The Substance is a must read for those who want to understand what daily faith is all about. Dr. Dennis Sempebwa takes you on a journey of faith through the lives of people in the Bible. Our Christian heritage and belief is built on faith in Jesus' finished work at Calvary. There is simply no such thing as an overdose of faith for the Christian. We know full well that's what we need in order to please God! Faith is not merely an option; it is a requirement in the Kingdom of God. That's why every day we fight the good fight of faith.

Peter M. Kairuz
CEO, Christian Broadcasting Network Asia, Manila, Philippines

I can say with all my heart that this book is fantastic! It gives the reader real access to the mystery of God!

Father Bernardo Francesco Gianni
The Basilica of San Miniato al Monte
Florence, Italy

Dr. Dennis Sempebwa has graced this earth for such a time as this! God allowed our paths to cross in Germany almost ten years ago and the Lord used this man of faith to speak destiny into this daughter of God. This gentle giant has penned a theological treatise with the simplicity of a servant. The church of today has all but abandoned the beauty of child-like faith, and replaced it with self-sufficiency and worldly counsel. We call the preacher expecting God for a multi-million dollar jet "full of faith," yet the precious soul on his knees, uncompromised, about to be martyred, we pity. What has happened to Biblical faith? Where are those who will put God to the test of His Word? *"Test Me now, says the Lord..."* (Malachi 3:10) The Substance, I believe, is a clarion call to get back to the basics—the foundations—of our faith. It is a trumpet that will blow across the nations of this world igniting a new, yet old, fire in the hearts of God's people to BLIND FAITH! An unfeigned faith that will grip the heart of Father God and move mountains! I don't know about you, but I BELIEVE!

Deborah G. Hunter
Author, "The Wilderness"and"The Call of Intercession"
Publisher (Hunter Heart Publishing)
Colorado Springs, CO U.S.A.

Many believers see faith as "heavenly-good," but not "earthly-necessary." If you are one of them, you are in for some blessed awakening. Read this book and you will see. YES, faith is very much a necessity in our everyday life! It is faith that "overcomes the world." (1 John 5:4) Thank you, Dr. Dennis, for writing this book. I am confident that it will stir up the body of Christ to walk in faith, in the small and great things of life.

Hiram G. Pangilinan
Senior Pastor, Church So Blessed International
Quezon City, Philippines

DEDICATION

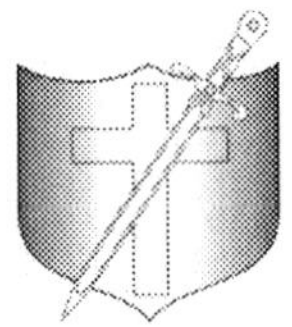

This book is dedicated to the poor,
the broken-hearted, the captives, the blind and the bruised among us – those to whom our Lord Jesus Christ was sent. (Luke 4:18)

ACKNOWLEDGEMENTS

To my precious wife and number one cheerleader, Ingrid—thank you for loving me, nurturing our amazing babies and for traveling this often-treacherous journey with me.

To our lovely “Chocolates" Adam, Abigail, Caleb, Judah and Elijah. I’m honored that you guys call me “Daddy”. Love you immeasurably.

To my incredible mother, Deborah, and my brothers and sisters—I love you all.

To Faith Ayida, Eric & Anne Kimunyu, and our daughter Abigail Sempebwa for helping me transcript the original manuscript. Your gifts were a tremendous blessing.

To my publisher Deborah Hunter. Thank you for believing in this vision. I’m honored to be counted among your counsel of confidence.

To Dean and Lisa Romesburg, for the gift of friendship. Thank you for loving us so unselfishly.

To John and Judy Van Wagoner, and Cam and Jeanne Cameron, for helping me make this vision a reality. May the Lord satisfy you with a long and prosperous life! Thank you!

To our missionary teams both in the U.S.A. and around the world. Thank you for walking with me. It is a great honor to serve with you all.

Finally, to all my spiritual fathers, spiritual sons, mentors, protégés, teachers, friends, associates and even enemies. Without you, I certainly would not be here. I bless you all!

TABLE OF CONTENTS

OPENING THOUGHT

Why write another book on faith? Don't we have enough already? Aren't our libraries and bookstores filled with volumes on this subject?

That is exactly what I thought when it became clear I was to write this book. I debated, deflected, and procrastinated until it began to burn within me.

I don't know whom God has in mind to read and grow from this, but here it is. And, I'll tell you what: jump to chapter one and judge for yourself. If it reads like some rhetorical treatise, theological rant or regurgitated dogmatic euphemisms on what I think to be the most important subject in the life of any believer, then please throw it in the trash and save your valuable time. As I have said many times, the world doesn't need another smart sermon, or an erudite doctrine, or another best-selling book for that matter. We have enough of that! And by the state of some of our churches, I doubt we have benefited by it.

If you agree with everything I have written, then I probably have missed the mark. My aim is not to please, appease or impress, but to stir. If you decide these truths deserve your time and attention, then by all means, give it. Allow the Holy Spirit to set your heart ablaze with His power, as you relish in "The mystery that has been kept hidden for ages and generations, but is now disclosed to the Lord's people ...Christ in you, the hope of glory" (Colossians 1:26, 27).

Chapter 1
A SIMPLE FAITH

"Verily I say unto you, Whosoever shall not receive the Kingdom of God as a little child, he shall in no wise enter therein."

Mark 10:15 (ASV)

I hail from the Baganda tribe in the East African nation of Uganda. We are the largest tribe in the country. Our main occupation is farming. In the morning, roosters wake us up—no alarm clocks here. With our primitive tools, we hit the *shambas,* or plantations, most of which have been in our families for generations. It's what we do—we are farmers. We toil in the sweltering hot morning African sun until we can't see our shadows anymore. When the sun is directly overhead, its lunchtime, time to take a break; it's too hot! So we find some shade, which is great because in that region of the continent, on the shores of the largest lake in Africa—Lake Victoria, you can always count on the gentle breeze to cool you down. Lunch normally consists of a cassava root wrapped in banana leaves. No, we don't have a cold bottle of water to chug down. In fact, clean water is hard to come by. Perhaps, like camels, we have learned to conserve our fluids. After lunch break, when you can see your shadow again, it's time for the afternoon shift to begin and back to the shamba we go—until the sun starts to set, then it's time to go home.

Everyone knows everyone else. Although we don't have Western comforts there, we have each other. We do struggles, joys, pain, hardships, family, and most of life together. This is the African village, and we love it!

On Sunday, some of us get to go to church.

It's an early day for almost every churchgoer. Except for a privileged few, we all walk to church; sometimes we walk for hours. For many, this is the only time we get to wear what we call *nice clothes*.

You must leave home early enough so you don't miss anything—for two reasons: first, you don't really know when you will be able to go to church again. With such a short life span and highly volatile environment, life here is indeed very unpredictable; every moment in God's presence is cherished as if it were the last. Second, we literally believe that church is a place where we meet with God. In other words, when we gather together we are assembled before a King; and not just any ordinary king. In our culture, it is unheard of to make a king wait. When a king is expected to visit a village, the natives literally line up for hours to anxiously await his arrival. We figure, if we do that for an earthly king, then what about the King of kings? Isn't His name, Jesus Christ - the *"King of kings and Lord of lords?"* (1 Timothy 6:15) I shall share more about this in Chapter Eleven.

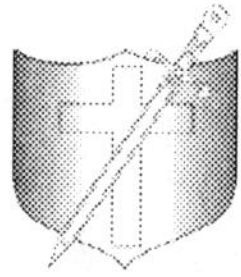

I still remember my glorious introduction to Jesus. I will never forget the day I first heard about "the good God of heaven, who gave His only Son to die for me!" Okay, that sounds ridiculous to my African mind, and I'll tell you why: first of all, we don't know of any good gods. African gods are mean, terrifying, demanding, and ruthless. Our gods extort from us: chickens, goats, and money. Whatever little we have, they want it for appeasement. When there's a pestilence or drought they might even demand human blood. Yes, some of us have had to give our sons so some lingering evil would abate. That's just how it is; our gods are just not loving. They don't give to us without a steep price.

Second, no father in his right mind would ever think about endangering the life of any of his sons for another. Fathers hope their sons will bear their legacies and maintain their bloodlines. They will gladly give their lives for their sons. So, in our culture, the notion that a father would slay his son for people he didn't even know is ludicrous. And if indeed He was such a powerful God—the God of all heaven and earth—why would He stoop so low for us here in Africa? Is he a desperate God? A weak God?

But, strangely, my introduction to Him was beautiful! All of it; the whole ridiculous story was beautifully romantic, intriguing, even inviting and somewhat convicting. The God we didn't know, shedding the blood of His only Son for us thousands of years ago?

So, the story draws us in. It climaxes with an invitation to simply accept its premise, and by doing so, enter its promise: eternal life!

And we do! And just like that, the story actually comes alive. Indeed it's true; the God of heaven and earth is a loving God. Jesus comes to dwell among us: a broken, desperately lost people! Almost immediately, it is clear He is not some weakling, by any means. He is, in fact, mightier than all our gods. Their representatives, the witches, had terrorized us for centuries. There was no doubt they were powerful. One witch doctor would float on a goatskin on Lake Victoria. Masses would gather to see him. Yet, even his god was no match for our God! Our God is a consuming fire.

> **God Never Asks Us To Understand His Ways. He Only Asks Us To Believe His Word!**

We fell in love with Him, gripped by the simplicity of it all. We didn't have to understand the story. In fact, He never asked us to. He simply wanted us to believe—to believe that two thousand years ago, our complete freedom had been purchased by the shed blood of His precious Son. Who can really understand that? God's ways are far beyond ours. He says, concerning His magnitude, that, "Heaven is My throne and the earth is My footstool." (Acts 7:49) How could we understand Him? Even if we tried, how could we possibly apprehend the magnificence of such a commanding and formidable God?

Still, as humans, it is our nature to try and understand. We naturally seek to understand before we will believe. And the more advanced a society is, the greater the compulsion for intellectual control. Advanced societies are typically intellectually astute. They tend to question anything that doesn't make logical sense, and will reject it until it does. Living in what is believed to be the most advanced society in the world, here in the U.S.A., I have seen this first hand.

Unfortunately for us, this human system of cognition is the antithesis of faith. We seek to understand before we believe; that's what comes naturally for us. But faith challenges us to flip it around. Faith seeks to believe before it understands; simply because we could never understand anyway. This thing—this story; our glorious Christian faith—was never meant to be understood, but simply believed.

Mark 10:13 says, *"And they brought young children to Him, that He should touch them: and His disciples rebuked those that brought them."*

Children Don't Need To Understand Before They Believe.

In other words, "Hey parents, I know you want Jesus to touch your kids, but let's not bother Him with this. He is really busy right now with the grownups, with the sick, destitute, and the needy. Please step aside!"

Jesus was not amused. He: *"...was much displeased, and said unto them, Suffer the little children to come unto Me, and forbid them not: for of such is the Kingdom of God."* (Mark 10:14)

One translation says Jesus was filled with indignation. He was irate that His disciples were trying to keep the kids away. Then He makes a profound statement:

> *"Suffer the little children to come unto to Me and forbid them not: for of such is the Kingdom of God. Verily I say unto you, whosoever shall not receive the Kingdom of God as a little child, he shall not enter therein."* (Mark 10:14, 15)

The Message Bible translation puts it this way: *"Unless you accept God's Kingdom in the simplicity of a child, you'll never get in."*

When she was younger, my daughter Abbey and I used to play what we called the "catch-me" game. She would get up on a table and jump into my arms, over and over again. She loved it, and I did too; even though it wore me out.

One morning, we were getting ready to leave the house, but she wanted to play "catch-me." Of course, I objected; we had places to go! Besides, I was physically too far away from her. Well, she insisted she wanted to play and proceeded to climb onto the kitchen table.

"Daddy, I'm jumping…jumping now," she announced with the biggest, most mischievous grin!

"Great, uh, but not now, honey," I dismissed.

She decided to count for me, "ONE!"

I thought she'd never jump. Her big brother, Adam, is very, very cautious. There is no way he'd jump without making doubly sure I would catch him. But Abbey was different—of course she was. What was I thinking, she is a girl! I didn't know just how markedly different those two species of humans were!

"TWO!" she continued to count. Nah, she couldn't. Surely she could see this was not an optimal situation. Surely she knew the velocity of the impact from her fall from that height, coupled with the distance between us, would present a challenge.

Abbey didn't seem to care …

"THREE!" And then she jumped!

I don't know to this day how I caught her, but I sure did. As soon as I placed her back on the table, it was time to have a stern conversation with my rambunctious daughter.

"Why did you do that? Couldn't you tell I was too far away?"

Abbey was looking up at me, smiling and somewhat confused. I could almost hear her thoughts:

> *"Daddy what's your problem? I thought I counted for you? Isn't that what we do—I jump and you catch me, right? It worked okay, and as a matter of fact, I think I really liked that a lot more than our normally short, safe jumps. I want to do that again, Daddy. Can we do that again, please?"*

I immediately calmed down and kissed her. My Abbey didn't need to understand the complexity of our game. She didn't need to explore the potential danger of a missed catch. All she knew was, every time she jumped Daddy would catch her no matter what. Abbey, as a kid, didn't need to figure out how I would catch her; and even if she wanted to, she simply couldn't. She hadn't yet developed the capacity to understand the physics of it all.

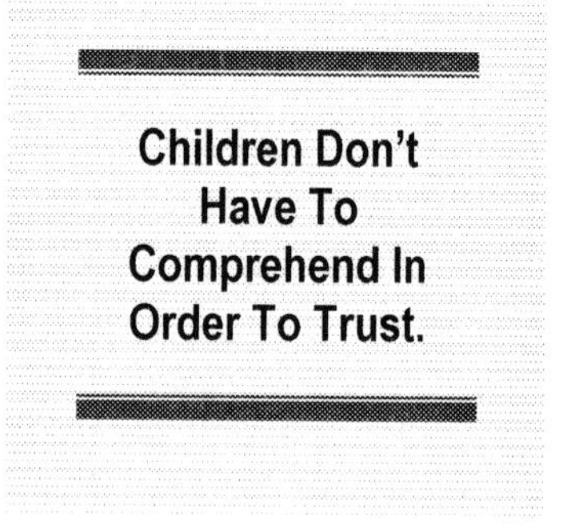

Children Don't Have To Comprehend In Order To Trust.

One defining trait of being a child is they don't need to understand before they believe. They know how to trust precisely because they don't need to understand how. To put it differently, they understand that they cannot understand.

Isaiah 55:8 says,

"For My thoughts are not your thoughts, nor are your ways My ways," says the LORD." (NKJV)

The New Living Translation puts it this way:

"My thoughts are nothing like your thoughts," says the Lord. "And My ways are far beyond anything you could imagine."

That's our God; He's not just some human father asking His daughter to trust him with her safety. No, our God is much, much bigger! His thoughts aren't ours; our ways aren't His! He asks us to trust Him like little children. Unless we put our understanding to the side and simply believe Him, we cannot enjoy His goodness; we cannot partake of His Kingdom.

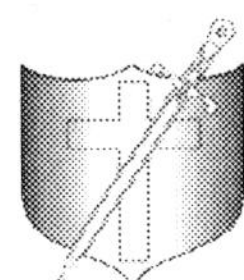

Months after I had accepted Christ, I volunteered to serve with the evangelism team at a mass crusade in Western Uganda. What a treat; I was completely blown away by the power of God as, night after night; we saw the most incredible miraculous healings, and deliverances from demons. Hundreds accepted Jesus as Lord!

So, as we were dismantling down the stage after the end of the final night, a woman walked up to me and said, "Will you please pray for us? We need a miracle."

Immediately I thought, *Dennis you can't. You are not qualified to do that just yet. You just came to attend and watch God touch a town.*

So, I looked around for a pastor or someone more trained for that kind of thing.

"My daughter and I have walked for hours," she continued. "I didn't know this was the final night. Please, you have to pray for us."

I thought, *Well, how bad could it be? I will just say a simple prayer and send them on their way. Maybe all they need is a blessing. That I can do…*

I said, "Sure ma'am, lets pray!"

Immediately, she shoved her daughter in front of me and said,

"There, you pray for her now!"

"Okay. What do you need for Jesus to do for her?" I asked.

"She can't see!"

My head started spinning. I was thinking, *Oh no! I really need a pastor for this one. I was hoping for a small issue, like a tummy ache or migraine headache. But blindness—no way, that's for experts!*

The woman closed her eyes, and waited for me to begin.

Then I thought, *I'll just pray a real quick quiet prayer and walk away, never to see her again. Jesus, you have to help me please!*

I decided to touch her like I saw my pastor do all week. I placed my fingers over her eyes, but to my shock, they sunk deep into her skull. The girl had no eyeballs! Fear ripped through my body—*Why Lord? Why such a complex case*?—I lamented. But, I didn't want to show my shock.

Suddenly, faith began to rise up inside me. I knew it was impossible for me to help her, apart from the supernatural intervention of

God. This woman had walked miles to come to Jesus for healing for her daughter.

I prayed a prayer of faith:

"Jesus, I thank You for You're the same yesterday, today and forever. And You'll do what You did in the Bible-days. In Jesus' name, blind eyes open now!"

I took my hands off and suddenly the girl fell to the ground, holding her head as she rolled away, loudly moaning with pain. Her mother hovered over her ailing daughter as I looked for a place to hide.

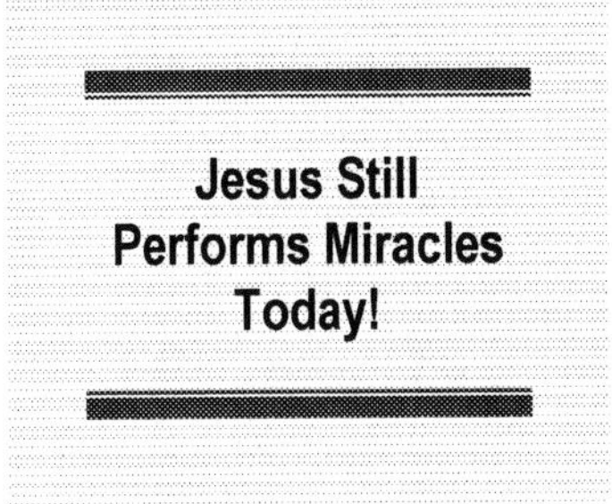
Jesus Still
Performs Miracles
Today!

What did I do, Lord? What happened? I thought.

"Ooooh!" the mother yelled.

She stood up and, with the biggest smile, began to dance. As she let out a celebratory African scream, I bent over to pick up her daughter. There they were: brilliant brown eyes! She was having trouble opening them because she had never seen light. That explained the painful wriggle moments earlier—Jesus had given her brand new eyeballs.

"Thank you, sir. I knew that was going to happen!" said the woman as she walked away. What? She knew her daughter would be healed? Her words hit me really hard. She simply believed! The writer of Hebrews defines faith as:

"The substance of things hoped for, the evidence of things not seen." (Hebrews 11:1)

This is where we get the title of this book.

Faith is the assurance that what we hope for shall manifest in reality. The Amplified Bible concludes that faith perceives as a *"real fact what is not revealed to the senses."* That's powerful! This woman said she knew her daughter would get healed, so she walked miles to come and receive the manifestation of her hope. The miracle happened, not because I had such a powerful healing anointing or because I was some accomplished healing minister, but as a result of this mother's simple faith!

Faith Perceives As A Real Fact, What Is Not Revealed To The Senses.

Matthew concludes, *"And said, 'Verily I say unto you, Except ye be converted, and become as little children, ye shall not enter into the kingdom of heaven.'" (Matthew 18: 3)*

Jesus doesn't say, "Hey it might help you get into heaven if you believe as a kid." Rather, He says, "… you SHALL NOT enter…" He leaves no option for us.

The good news is we can be converted and become like children. This is the backbone of Biblical faith. It is simple, because it really cannot be anything else. The title of this chapter is somewhat redundant because, in reality, there is no such thing as complicated faith. All true faith is simple and uncomplicated!

Real Faith Is Simple And Uncomplicated.

A final note to those who have journeyed with Christ awhile: we can become simple again. This verse applies to the babes and the spiritually mature. The Spirit of God is calling us to return to maturity.

Chapter Truths
A SIMPLE FAITH

1. **God Never Asks Us To Understand His Ways. He Only Asks Us To Believe His Word.**

2. **Children Don't Need To Understand Before They Believe.**

3. **Children Don't Have To Comprehend In Order To Trust.**

4. **Jesus Still Performs Miracles Today!**

5. **Faith Perceives As A Real Fact, What Is Not Revealed To The Senses.**

6. **Real Faith Is Simple And Uncomplicated.**

Chapter 2
A VALIANT FAITH

"And He said unto them,
'Why are ye so fearful?
How is it that ye have no faith?'"

Mark 4:40

Jesus was probably exhausted. He had been teaching all day, touching the broken and ministering to the needy. He turned to His beloved disciples and said:

> *"'Let's cross to the other side of the lake.' So they took Jesus in the boat and started out, leaving the crowds behind (although other boats followed). But soon a fierce storm came up. High waves were breaking into the boat, and it began to fill with water."* (Mark 4: 35-37, NLT)

The New King James version says, *"... a great windstorm arose."* The Greek word interpreted here as "windstorm" is *Lilaps*. This word literally means a ferocious storm that breaks suddenly from black thunderclouds, in furious gusts with punishing rain. Other words we could use are "hurricane" or "typhoon".

The other interesting word used there, "arose," is the Greek word *ginomai.* This word means something that completely blindsides you, something that happens unexpectedly, catching one completely off guard. This was the picture: blue sky, no violent weather in the forecast, everything looked great, and all of a sudden in the middle of the sea—BOOM! Out of nowhere came this fierce gale with one hundred mile-per-hour winds. The boat began to fill with water. There were no rescue boats, no coast guard, and no help! There is no mention of what became of the other smaller boats in their entourage, but boy, they were all in trouble!

Friends, have you ever done exactly what God asked you to do, and instead of experiencing peace, joy, and goodness, you were pummeled by a typhoon? This is one of the most confusing things for Christians; to obey God, to do what Jesus asked you to do and instead of blessings you encounter devastation and hardship—a ferocious storm.

Jim takes excellent care of his body. He sleeps well, exercises, eats well, but all of a sudden his system is in a free-fall. He has developed all kinds of medical complications. "What happened, Lord?" He is fighting a storm in the middle of the sea and his boat is filling fast!

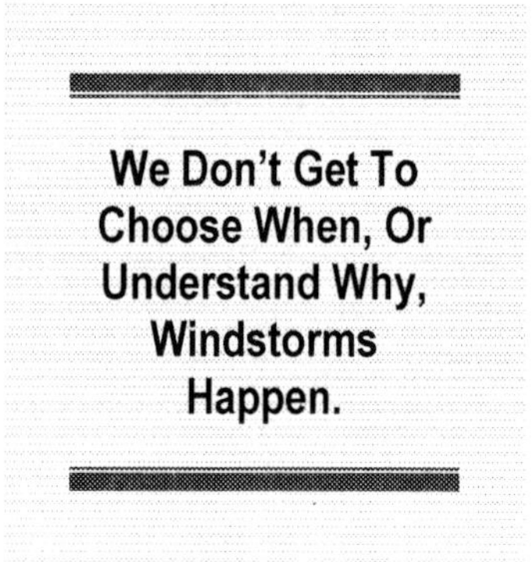

We Don't Get To
Choose When, Or
Understand Why,
Windstorms
Happen.

Rita is a virgin. She has been waiting on the Lord for her perfect Mr. Right, and she believes Randall is the one. All her friends, family, and even her pastor agree. She is determined to shout the virtues of patience upon the mountaintops when suddenly, right before their wedding, Randall is diagnosed with stage four cancer. Her beloved fiancé has only three months to live. She is fighting a storm in the middle of the sea and her boat is filling fast!

We don`t get to choose when, and rarely do we even understand why, storms happen. I speak with hundreds of people every year who bemoan, "Pastor, I don`t know why this is happening to me."

"Why did I get fired?"

"Why did my husband leave me?"

"Why is our business collapsing?"

"Why are my kids rebelling?"

"Why is my best friend trying to destroy me?"

Why, why, why? I call this being stuck on *Why Avenue*. And in a culture obsessed with knowledge and information, there is no wonder why *Why Avenue* is super congested.

If I may ask, what if you never find out why? Then what? Do you just give up and capsize? What if out of all your super-healthy siblings, you are the only one struggling with chronic illnesses? And, okay, let's say one day you get to know why. Then what? Will that help fix you? Is there really an acceptable "why" to the loss of your only child, the collapse of your marriage, or the rape of your sister?

Instead of fixating on your un-fixable dilemma, remember *who* is in your boat. Remember who told you to come this way. Remember Jesus!

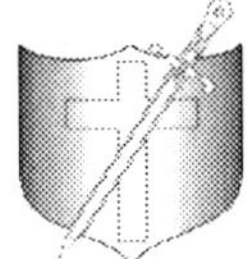

And that is exactly what His disciples did.

But there was a problem: *"Jesus was in the stern, sleeping on a cushion."* (Mark 4:38a, NIV)

What? Jesus was deep asleep in the middle of a typhoon? They figured He needed to be reminded of their predicament; or maybe He wasn't even concerned.

"The disciples woke Him up, shouting, "Teacher, don't You care that we're going to drown?" (Mark 4:38b, NLT)

Friends, a real windstorm will make you do two things:

1) Forget who you are

As the storms beat upon their frail boat, Peter and his crew probably felt like mere fishermen again; like dying mortals. They didn't feel like emissaries and confidants to the Son of God. For a second there, they lost sight of who they were, and, most importantly, *whose* they were.

2) Forget the plan

Jesus never said, "Guys, let's see if we can cross over to the other side." He said with certainty, "Let's cross over!" But *Lailaps* makes them forget the plan, as such storms often do.

When life throws us a curveball, when things hit us so hard in the face, the first real casualty is our confidence. We feel mortal, perishable, and become so consumed by the magnitude of the storm that we forget we are the King's kids!

A True Windstorm Is Always Equal To Your Constitution. It Will Test You To The Limit.

John writes, *"...greater is He that is in you, than he that is in the world."* (1 John 4:4)

> *"Then he arose and rebuked the wind and said to the sea, 'Peace! Be still.' The wind ceased, and there was great calm."* (Mark 4:39, NKJV)

As you can imagine, the guys were all probably drenched from one of the toughest fights of their lives. For what seemed like forever, they'd been trying to empty the boat to save it from sinking. Then, suddenly, there was deafening silence and serenity. Perhaps Jesus ought to appreciate their noble, though failed, efforts to protect Him. But the Master had a different perspective all together: this was a teaching moment, which could not be wasted. He must address their failings and help equip them for many such storms that would surely come.

> *"Why are you so fearful? How is it that you have no faith? Do you still have no faith in Me?"* (Verse 40, NKJV)

I always had a problem understanding the disappointment Jesus had with His faithful disciples. Internally, I thought, "Jesus, why blame the guys for being afraid? How could they not be? Were they not supposed to face the facts of their predicament?" But Jesus was after something different. His issue wasn't that their quandary wasn't scary, but that they would allow it to speak louder to them than the presence of their Master. "Why did you forget the plan?" Why did you listen to the storm? Why did you forget ME?"

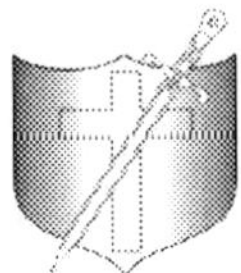

Three lessons from this story:

1. Windstorms are unavoidable.

After hearing me speak about this for almost all his life, my son Adam coined a phrase: "You are either in a storm or headed into one." How true that is! As long as you are living, storms will hit you; stuff will happen. You might lose a business, suffer chronic illness, and need to bail your son out of jail, or bury your only child. I have lived an existence that didn't know life without tragedy.

You Are Either Coming Out Of A Windstorm, Or Headed Right Into One!

Jesus promises: *"...In the world ye shall have tribulation..."* (John 16:33a)

The Greek word interpreted here as "tribulations" is *Thlipsis*. This word means circumstances so dire, one feels completely squeezed, stressed, pressured, or crushed. Yikes! Yes, along with abundant life, exceeding joy, and inexplicable peace that passes all understanding, we are told to expect crushing, pressing, squeezing, and stressful circumstances—*Thlipsis*. So, what do we do with that? Freak out? Let's read the prescription Jesus gave:

*"... but be of good cheer; I have overcome the world." (*John 16:33b)

Interesting that He doesn't say, "Be of good cheer, I'll save you from them." Instead, He encourages us to be joyful because He has overcome.

2. Windstorms are temporary.

I remember the tedious process of encouraging our toddlers to take those first baby steps. Over and over they would fall down and even hurt themselves in their attempts to walk. But not once did my wife or I say, "Okay, Adam, you've had your chance and blown it. Lesson over. Don't try that again." On the contrary, we encouraged them to try again and again, until they learned to not only walk, but also to run.

The Portuguese have a saying: "Stumbling is not falling." In fact, show me a person who has never stumbled, and I will show you someone who has never attempted to walk. Does one drown because they fall into water? No, they drown because they refuse or fail to get out. Proverbs 24:10 says, *"If thou faint in the day of adversity, thy strength is small."*

What does that mean to me? There is a day that brings adversity; but like every other day, it ends at some point. Stormy days come and go. They are not permanent.

However Fierce They Are, All Windstorms Eventually Blow Over.

3. Windstorms reveal who we are.

Poet Titus Lucretius Carus writes: "Look at a man in the midst of doubt and danger, and you will learn in his hour of adversity what he really is!" That is precisely what windstorms do: they reveal who we are, and what we are made of.

The late author Zig Ziglar told a story of a man who had just visited the *Biosphere Two*, a man-made habitat in Arizona. This is a structure where scientists attempted to artificially grow plant life. Initially, the designers had a big problem: their trees would grow to a certain height and then topple over from their weight. Finally, they figured out the designers had made a critical oversight: they needed to create wind within the structure. Without wind, the trees could not grow a strong enough root system to hold their weight. It is the wind that helped them create that deeply extended root system.

4. Windstorms reveal whose you are.

How do you absolutely know Jesus heals? From Bible stories, sermons or testimonies of others? Until you are deathly sick and experience His power first hand, you have never met Jesus the Healer! Until you are besieged by adversaries committed to destroying you, you don't really know Jesus the Deliverer. For years, I read about God's delivering Hand through the Old Testament. Inasmuch as I was inspired, it was more theoretic to me until my family was encompassed and stalked by folks whose primary aim was to destroy us. Then I really saw God's delivering Hand.

Hosea 2:14 says:

"Therefore, behold, I will allure her,
Will bring her into the wilderness,
And speak comfort to her."(NKJV)

Your Windstorm Carries A Gift. Make Sure You Unwrap It Even While You Weep.

What a beautiful verse! Sometimes, God will invite you into a wilderness so He can speak to you. My friend Deborah Hunter has published a wonderful book on the subject. She says,

"Each of us will encounter a wilderness experience at least once in our lives. We must embrace these times of great testing in order to walk fully into the promise of God for our lives. You are in great company: David, Elijah, Samson, Solomon, Deborah, Job, and yes, even our Lord and Savior Jesus Christ—each walked though their

own wildernesses in order that we, too, can get to the other side of ours." [1]

A wilderness is a place that is:

- difficult
- dry
- frigid
- dangerous
- lonely
- dark
- desolate
- cold

Peter comes to church as a tradition. He never misses. Well, except on those Sundays when the weather is really nice. You see, that's when he gets to take his family to the beach. Oh, and, of course, when it's really cold outside, he and his family find it much cozier to settle in to the comfort of their living room and watch some Christian TV. This is his thing: convenient Christianity. Well, until he loses his job. The shock sends him right back to church. See, he really needs Jesus now. He arrives thirty minutes before service starts because now he has time to volunteer as a greeter. Now he never misses an evening service, even though he never attended one before. His Monday mornings are much different, too. Peter never used to speak about Jesus because it was kind of embarrassing. He preferred to be a closet Christian. Now that he has to go stand in line at the unemployment office, he gets to see suffering people; people with no hope at all, not like him. At least he has a graduate degree and lots of experience; it is unlikely that he won't soon land something. For the first time, he is compelled to share his faith. Clearly, his windstorm was an invitation by God into the wilderness where his faith has now been renewed.

---

[1] Hunter, Deborah G. *The Wilderness, A Place of Preparation.* Colorado Springs: Hunter Heart Publishing, 2014.

I have friends who would never pray unless they were in dire straits. Many of us would never go to church if all was well with us. I'm not suggesting God wants to torture you to get you to pay attention to Him; I am only saying what the Bible says: God will often call us to difficult spaces in order to speak to us.

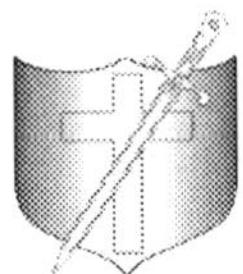

Verse 41 concludes, *"The disciples were absolutely terrified. "Who is this man?" they asked each other. "Even the wind and waves obey Him!"(NLT)*

One translation actually says, "What kind of man is this?" That reminds me of a little chorus we used to sing way back in Africa with these words: "*Omusajja namabky'oyo Halleluya*!" Translated, What kind of man is this…Halleluya."

We'd sing this over and over, giving glory to His wondrous acts.

Gaze Into The Darkness Of Your Windstorm Long Enough, And You Shall Clearly See His Immaculate Light.

Indeed, His disciples had seen Him perform miracles for others but until they saw Him speak to the wind, they really didn't know Him. This was a Jesus they'd never met. Until Jesus raises you up from that deathbed, rescues you from an epidemic, or restores your dead marriage, you don't really know Him that way!

Annie Johnson Flint writes: [2]

Have you come to the Red Sea place in your life,
Where in spite of all you can do,

---

[2] Johnson-Flint, Annie. *"Red Sea"*. Graphics and background by Mary Vannattan http://www.homemakerscorner.com/ajf-redsea.htm. 5 Sept. 2015

There is no way out,
There is no way back,
There is no other way but through?

Then wait on the Lord with a trust serene;
Till the night of your fear is gone;
He will send the wind,
He will heap the floods;
When He says to your soul, "Go on."

And His hand will lead you through - clear through -
Ere the watery walls roll down,
No foe can reach you, no wave can touch,
No mightiest sea can drown;

The tossing billows may rear their crests,
Their foam at your feet may break,
But over their bed you shall walk dryshod
In the path that your Lord will make.

In the morning watch, 'neath the lifted cloud,
You shall see but the Lord alone.
When He leads you on from the place of the sea;
To a land you have not known;

And your fears shall pass as your foes have passed,
You shall no more be afraid;
You shall sing His praise in a better place,
A place that His hand has made.

My friends, faith is audacious: it lives today, right now, courageously with foresight that can only be understood in hindsight. There is no telling what God can do until you come through to the other side. Can you stare your storm in the face and say, "Okay, c'mon, bring it on! No matter what you do, it shall be well with me"? Do you have valiant faith?

Chicago attorney Horatio Spafford was blessed with a beautiful wife and five kids. With a thriving business, he was one of the richest men of his day…until tragedy hit. First, his only son suddenly passed away. Then, he lost everything in The Great Chicago Fire of 1871. Three years later, he was done with America. Before he and his family boarded the French ship "Villa de Havre" bound for England, he was held back to attend to some urgent business. He decided to send his wife and four daughters ahead. Tragically, the ship sank. After weeks of anguish, he received a telegraph from England from his wife with two words, SAVED ALONE! All his daughters had perished in the disaster. As he traveled to England to join his precious wife, he penned this classic hymn: [3]

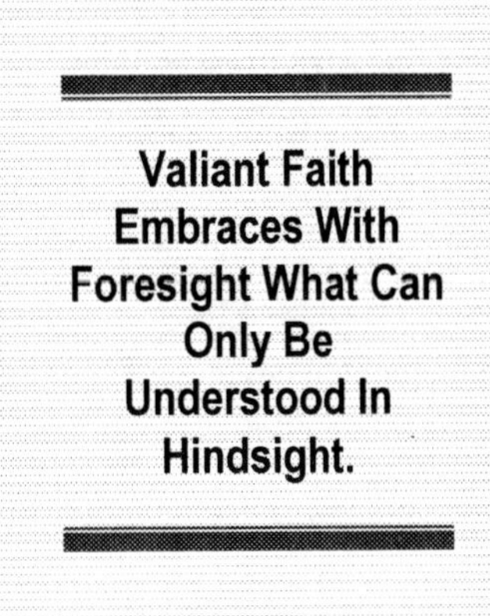
Valiant Faith Embraces With Foresight What Can Only Be Understood In Hindsight.

When peace, like a river, attendeth my way,
When sorrows like sea-billows roll;
Whatever my lot, Thou hast taught me to say,
"It is well, it is well with my soul."

Though Satan should buffet, though' trials should come,
Let this blest assurance control,
That Christ has regarded my helpless estate,
And hath shed His own blood for my soul.

My sin, oh, the bliss of this glorious thought!
My sin, not in part, but the whole,
Is nailed to the cross and I bear it no more,
Praise the Lord, praise the Lord, O my soul.

And, Lord haste the day, when my faith shall be sight,

---

3 Spafford, Horatio. *"It Is Well With My Soul."* http://www.spaffordhymn.com/. 5 Sept 2015

The clouds be rolled back as a scroll;
The trump shall resound and the Lord shall descend
Even so, it is well with my soul.

It is well,
With my soul,
It is well; it is well, with my soul.

Chapter Truths
A VALIANT FAITH

1. **We Don't Get To Choose When, Or Understand Why, Windstorms Happen.**

2. **A True Windstorm Is Always Equal To Your Constitution. It Will Test You To The Limit.**

3. **You Are Either Coming Out Of A Windstorm, Or Headed Right Into One!**

4. **However Fierce They Are, All Windstorms Eventually Blow Over.**

5. **Your Windstorm Carries A Gift. Make Sure You Unwrap It Even While You Weep.**

6. **Gaze Into The Darkness Of Your Windstorm Long Enough, And You Shall Clearly See His Immaculate Light.**

7. **Valiant Faith Embraces With Foresight What Can Only Be Understood In Hindsight.**

Chapter 3
A FERVENT FAITH

"But he went out, and began to publish it much, and to blaze abroad the matter."

Mark 1:45

Mark 1:40 says, *"And there came a leper to Him, beseeching Him, and kneeling down to Him, and saying unto Him, 'If Thou wilt, Thou canst make me clean.'"*

Leprosy is a horribly disfiguring disease. According to the Law of Moses, lepers were unclean and all social interaction with them was strictly forbidden. They were permanently quarantined in leper's colonies beyond city outskirts. Imagine the pain of having a relative whom you'd never hug, kiss, or even touch. Imagine being labeled a curse in a tightly knit community.

This outcast heard about Jesus the healer. He knew that in order to get noticed by Jesus, he would have to leave the colony, or wherever he was hidden, risk his life by unlawfully mingling with a bunch of healthy people, and somehow attend the meeting where Jesus was. He had a choice: stay safe and remain chronically sick, or risk it all and go for the healing he so desperately desired.

He chose to go for the healing!

Once he saw Jesus, he fell down to his knees before Him and, crying out, presented his plea. Once again,

'If Thou wilt, Thou canst make me clean.'" (Mark 1:40b)

Let's unpack this picture for a second.

First, this is an *earnest* cry. The Greek work used there is *parakaleo*. It indicates a deep sense of pleading; more like, "Please Jesus, I beg of You …"

Second, this is a *reverent* cry. His posture is one of brokenness. In many cultures, kneeling is a sign of true respect, devotion and sincere admiration.

Third, this is a *humble* cry. *"If You will."* There is no presumption of entitlement here.

Fourth, this is a *believing* cry. *"... You can make me clean."* It is that assurance that I am certain inspired him to put himself out in such a manner. He was a man of faith. It isn't Jesus' ability to heal that is the issue, but His willingness. "Are You willing to heal me, Jesus?" not, "Are You able?"

Fifth, this cry is *specific*. He didn't say, "I am sure You can tell from my scars what I need Lord." Rather he said, "Jesus, make me clean." In other words, "Remove this curse from me."

Sixth, this cry is *personal*. "Make me clean." Or, "Jesus I am here because I have a deeply, personal, specific need from You. I want to get healed."

God Is Not Shocked By Your Predicament. He Knew About It Even Before You Prayed About It.

Finally, this cry is *brief*. In fact, in the Greek, the man's entire plea is represented in five words. Not some lengthy, *"Oh Jesus, I want You to know just how much I have suffered. I have no friends and no real life at all. Everyone treats me horribly. Sure, I know I am cursed, but must life be so hard? Now, I ask You, please sir, to find it in Your heart to touch this humble sinner."*

Do you ever feel like giving God a lecture about your predicament, as if He is unaware of it? Did you ever try to brief Him on your pain, to really let Him know how bad you feel or how dire your circumstance is? Well, I have. Funny how we think the louder, more colorful, expressive, or eloquent we are, the more God will understand us and more hastily come to our aid. Friends, God already knows.

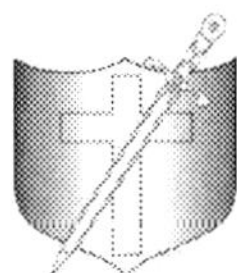

"When He saw and heard the man's cry, Jesus was moved with compassion." (Verse 41) The Greek word used there is the word *splagchnizomai*, which means, "to feel deep sympathy for". Jesus is moved with compassion. His response wasn't just: "Oh, hey guy; I suppose I can help you." It was more like: "Son, I really, really get you. In fact, I actually feel your shame, rejection, isolation, fear, and discouragement. I hurt for you!" Jesus is completely, deeply empathetic.

When we hit life's storms or tragedies, the temptation is to gather people around us to make us feel better about ourselves. We tend to send out invitations to our pity parties. I get it. It is natural to want people to comfort us, to yearn for that someone, even if it's only one person, who will tell us this thing is not going to kill us; that the storm shall soon pass. And how many of us have been left hanging and disappointed after some riotous pity party? You thought your friends would help. You thought they would numb your pain for you; and why not? That is, after all, what friends are for, right? Wrong!

A friend once sorrowfully said to me, "Dennis, I thought my friend cared. I told him how my entire world had come crashing down, and all he said was, 'Wow, that's bad. Can we eat? I am hungry.' That, after I had just told him how I had lost my job, how my daughter was deathly sick in the hospital and how my wife was struggling with depression. 'Let's eat'? Am I missing something here?"

Friends, Jesus is not that way at all. Jesus actually deeply understands us. He gets us, even before we say anything to Him.

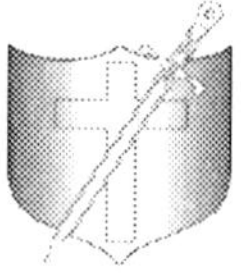

Jesus: *"... put forth His hand and touched him..."* (Verse 41b)

I can almost hear the loud gasps of shock and sheer unbelief, "Did Jesus just touch a leper?" That was taboo in that culture, as it was strictly forbidden by the Law of Moses. Remember, Jesus was a teacher and that very act would make him ritually unclean. He didn't seem concerned by the taboo or the Law itself. His only focus was the man's healing. In fact, not only did He touch him, Jesus spoke directly to him. He said, *"I will, be thou clean."*

In other words, "Yes, you're right My son; I am willing and I will make you clean. So ... *be thou clean."*

And as soon as he'd spoken, verse 42 says,

> *"...immediately the leprosy departed from him, and he was cleansed."*

Could Jesus have healed him without the touch? Of course. In fact, I am not even sure it was the touch that did it. I believe it was the command—His word—that healed him. The touch was simply to let him know, *"My son, although others may never understand what it is like to be a leper; to feel what you feel, to carry your load, your burden and your cross; I do. I get it. I really get it."*

No One Can Really Understand What You Are Going Through.

Someone is probably saying, "But people don't understand my shame, my pain, my disfigurement." Well, you are right, indeed they don't. Someone else might say, "But it seems like my family doesn't get it that I'm really broken and I am really hurt." Well, they kinda don't. As a matter of fact, they can't. The fact is we are all more attentive to our own pain than we are to others'. In other words, it is only to the extent we can defer our own pain, that we give ear to someone else's.

Do you honestly want to live your life jumping from one pity party to the next? How long do you intend to enable your addiction to sympathy? I know folk who will even exaggerate their pain or afflictions just so they get more sympathy. Friend, you don't have to. Be free now, in the name of Jesus. You don't have to reach out to a single human being. I want to tell you Jesus fully understands and He's willing to touch you. He's willing to heal you; He's willing to make you completely whole.

So, He healed the man. Can you imagine his joy? Can you imagine his excitement, his thrill?

> "*Yes! Yes! Yes! I'm healed, I'm whole; I'm healed, I'm whole! I'm healed. It worked, it worked, it worked! My plan worked. I knew if I'd get myself to this meeting, I knew if I'd get in front of this Jesus, I knew if I'd get His attention, Jesus would heal me!*"

He must have been just beyond himself. But Jesus wasn't done yet.

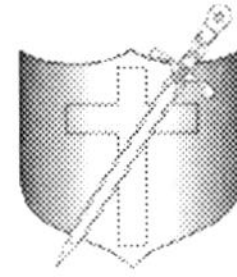

Verse 43-44 says,

> *"And he straitly charged him, and forthwith sent him away. And saith unto him, 'See thou say nothing to any man: but go thy way, shew thyself to the priest, and offer for thy cleansing those things which Moses commanded, for a testimony unto them."*

I can imagine his response:

> "*Priest. Yes, I can certainly do that. They will verify that I am well, that You have miraculously set me free from a curse. Be-*

> *sides, when I show up to visit with my family, I don't want them running for cover, thinking I am still infectious. So, yes, I can definitely do that. I need to do that!*
>
> *"Sacrifice. Offering. Absolutely, I am beyond grateful to God. Not a problem at all there, Jesus. I shall prepare my best and offer it to the Lord for a thank-offering.*
>
> *"But ... um ... that first one is going to be an issue, Jesus. You just restored my dignity, gave me back my health and brand-new identity, offered me an opportunity to live a normal life again, and now You're asking me not to tell anyone about it?"*

He did not obey Jesus' instruction. In fact, he did the opposite.

> *"But he went out and began to publish it much, and to blaze abroad the matter insomuch that Jesus could no more openly enter the city, but was without in desert places: and they came to Him from every quarter."(Mark 1:45)*

The Greek word for "publish" here is *keruso*. The term is used to reference a royal herald or announcement, which is exactly what the man did: "Here ye one and all. I was a leper, an outcast, but now I am healed." The Bible says, *"He went out, he began to publish it much and to blaze abroad the matter."*

To *blaze* means to incessantly, passionately, even *obsessively* spread abroad the matter. He did it so much that, *"Jesus could no more openly enter the city but was without in desert places."*

Well, he completely disobeyed Jesus' instruction. He didn't just tell a few folk; he didn't keep the news to his family; he didn't just confide in his old friends. He told everyone! And he did it so effectively that Jesus could no more openly enter the city.

Now, one could argue, as some scholars do, that this man's zeal was misplaced; that perhaps it hindered Jesus' ministry. I want to say that this man had Fervent Faith! You know the kind that cannot be contained. I've heard people say, "Dennis, I've been a Christian for about four years and you know last week I finally was able to tell my friends and co-workers." As much as I want to rejoice with them, I am thinking, *Whoa! Wait, wait a minute; you've been a Christian for how long? You mean for four years, you hadn't yet found an opportunity to talk about this Jesus who rescued you from eternal damnation, gave you hope and a future and the very meaning of life?*

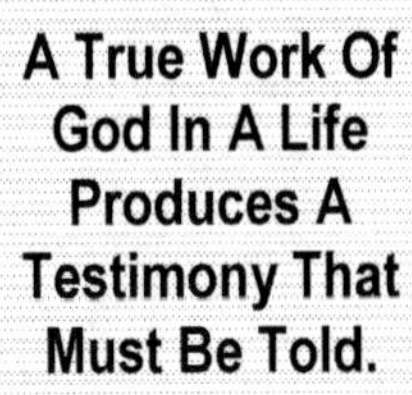

A True Work Of
God In A Life
Produces A
Testimony That
Must Be Told.

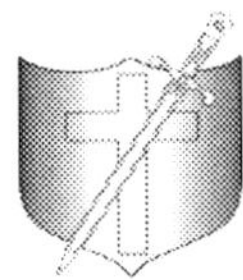

Guys, ours is not a closet faith. We're called to a fervent faith, a shameless faith. How could you possibly be quiet about what God has done for you, about His delivering work in your life?

Again, our take-away lessons from this story:

1. Jesus is absolutely, completely and always able. Paul declares:

   "Now unto Him that is able to do exceedingly abundantly above all that we ask or think, according to the power that worketh in us, Unto Him be glory in the church by Christ Jesus throughout all ages, world without end. Amen." (Ephesians 3:20, 21)

2. Jesus is compassionate. Yes, He cares. He doesn't just look at you from some exalted place. That's why He came in the flesh, and lived this crazy earthly life you and I are living now. Jesus lived here on earth so He can experience our pains, be tempted

like you and I, and still overcome like you and I should. The Bible says, *"This High Priest of ours understands our weaknesses, for He faced all of the same testings we do, yet He did not sin."* (Hebrews 4:15 NLT)

Gaze Into The Darkness Of Your Windstorm; There You Shall Clearly See The Hand Of God.

3. Once Jesus has moved in our lives, we just can't help but share it. His love is contagious. It's kind of like falling in love. Can you really keep it quiet? Don't we burn inside to share it from the mountaintops? Paul says in Romans 1:16, *"For I am not ashamed of the gospel of Christ: for it is the power of God unto salvation..."*

Chapter Truths
A FERVENT FAITH

1. God Is Not Shocked By Your Predicament. He Knew About It Even Before You Prayed About It.

2. No One Can Really Understand What You Are Going Through.

3. A True Work of God In A Life Produces A Testimony That Must Be Told.

4. Gaze Into The Darkness Of Your Windstorm; There You Shall Clearly See The Hand of God.

Chapter 4
A PERSISTENT FAITH

"And she said, Truth, Lord: yet the dogs eat of the crumbs which fall from their masters' table."

Matthew 15:27

> *"And behold a woman from Canaan came out to the same coasts and cried unto Him."* (Matthew 15:22a)

This poor woman was doubly disadvantaged. First, she was a Canaanite, a Gentile despised by the Jews. Second, she was a woman in a patriarchal society. Notwithstanding, she had need; her daughter had an incurable condition—she was afflicted by a demon. We can safely assume she had probably tried everything to get her cured.

She did something which, while bold, was very embarrassing. This outcast, Gentile woman raised her voice in a large gathering of Jews.

> *"Have mercy on me, O Lord, Thou Son of David; my daughter is grievously vexed with a devil." (Matthew 15:22b)*

It's interesting how she addressed him as the "Son of David", a designation reserved exclusively for the Messiah, the deliverer of the people of Israel. Not, "Please Jesus, healer of Nazareth," or "Jesus, Master and Teacher." She pleaded the mercies of the Promised One, the Son of David! Her declaration also meant she recognized His unlimited ability to help her, His capacity as the God-man, sent to deliver Israel from captivity.

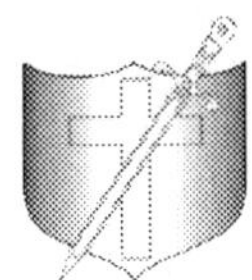

I imagine she felt pretty great when Jesus turned His head. "Yes! I have His attention now. Surely He will have mercy on me!" Unfortunately, that's not what happened. Verse 23 says, *"But He answered her not a word."*

I can almost feel her devastation. All that effort, courage, and the nerve it took to speak out, got her nothing; Jesus completely ignored her. She must have been mortified. She should just go away. She should retreat and cry in shame, and suffer her daughter's endless torment.

Think about the context for a second: Jesus the healer is there. He is probably surrounded by crowds of needy people, admirers, critics, zealots and poor people. Then out came the lone plea from a Gentile woman. She was really out of place.

The Intensity Of Your Adversity Dictates The Strength Of Your Desperation.

> *"And the disciples came and besought Him saying, 'Send her away for she cries after us.'"* One translation says, *"She's bothering us with all her begging."* In other words, "Jesus, can You just tell her where to go? Please get rid of her. She is upsetting us." Imagine her despair. As if it was not enough that her plea was unfruitful, Jesus' crew was urging Him to send her away.

But she was not about to leave; she was persistent!

Jesus finally spoke up, *"...I am not sent but unto the lost sheep of the house of Israel."* (Verse 24b)

In essence: "Uh, lady, I understand you have a need but I can't help you. I came for a special people—the Jews!"

Wham, another hit! First of all Jesus ignored her, and when He finally spoke up, He actually told her He didn't come for her "kind." She should just leave, right? Wouldn't you?

Not a chance—she was persistent!

Instead of drawing away or pulling back, she pushed further in to Jesus: *"Then came she and worshipped Him, saying, 'Lord, help me.'"* (Verse 25)

She was really saying: "Hey, okay, okay. I hear you. But sir, I don't think you understand just how desperate I am. No, I am not leaving. I can't just walk away." Her desperate eyes begged for an answer. She would not leave; she had to get help for her daughter. She didn't have the luxury of self-consciousness or embarrassment. She didn't care about protocol, norms or rules. It didn't matter that she did not qualify for Jesus' attention.

Imagine the staring eyes; they were hoping she'd leave. Imagine the whispers, "Wow! She sure has guts, I'd say. Even after Jesus responds to her failed entreaty, this Gentile woman still remains? Let's get on with it, Jesus; You've got more important people to attend to."

God Forbid We Walk Away From Our Breakthroughs On Account Of Human Opinion.

Jesus spoke again, *"It isn't right to take the children's bread and toss it to the dogs."* (Mark 15:26, NKJV)

In other words, *the reason I can't help you is you just don't qualify. I mustn't take these special blessings, meant for special people, and give it to those who aren't special. I cannot give this to a Gentile dog*. You see, the Jews referred to Gentiles as dogs. It was a derogative term, a racial slur, much like referring to African Americans as "niggers," or South African blacks as *kafiir*.

Now, that's bad, really bad. This woman should have gotten the point, right? She is not wanted, and now she knew precisely why. I can almost see the condescending crowd. This was just not her day. She should have listened to the crowd, to culture, to protocols and go back home to her ailing daughter.

But she had need, even though she was a dog. She was persistent!

She thought fast and responded to Jesus: *"Truth, Lord: yet the dogs eat of the crumbs which fall from their masters' table."*

Yes! I laugh every time I read this! In other words, "I agree with what You are saying Sir, but there is a way You can help me without altering Your plan. Yes, I am a dog, but as the House of Israel rejects Your food, let me catch some of the crumbs. I want the leftovers." Is she persistent, or what?

In what looks like a stunning flip-flop, Jesus says, "*O woman, great is thy faith..." (Verse 28)*

Can you imagine what the disciples were thinking? "What? I thought you agreed with us that she was a nuisance. We think you should have sent her away sooner. What changed?"

Persistent Faith Defies The Status Quo.

Persistent faith happened!

Jesus called her faith great because she defied the status quo. She defied the boundaries. She refused to go back to her "own kind." She pushed against the box. Thus, Jesus declared, *"'Be it unto thee even as thou wilt.' And her daughter was made whole from that very hour." (Verse 28)*

In other words, "Woman, what you wanted has been granted. Those demons have fled! Your crazy, persistent faith has made your daughter well!"

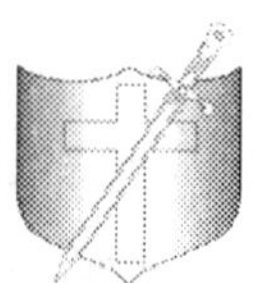

Persistent faith is option-less faith! It has no fall-back or plan B, thus it must attain its objective at any cost.

This is a marked difference between a person who comes to God with options and one who is completely out of them.

Persistent Faith Arouses Action To The Attainment Of Its Desired End.

Jesus says in Matthew 5:6:

> *"Blessed are they which do hunger and thirst after righteousness: for they shall be filled."*

Hunger is the compulsion to eat; to nourish. Thirst is a compulsion to hydrate; to drink. I know what hunger is, I know about going several days without food. I've never seen a comfortable, restful, thirsty man; or a rested, content, hungry woman. On the contrary! Hungry people have a sense of urgency; they are very uncomfortable. They are restless, they are very discontented. They persistently strive for immediate relief. Jesus is suggesting it is a persistent pursuit for righteousness that yields fruit and causes fulfillment.

James 2:17 says, *"Even so faith, if it hath not works, is dead, being alone."*

James advises that merely believing without action is the same as having dead faith. Just talking, trusting, yearning, desiring, wanting and even believing for something doesn't do anything for you. Faith must have corresponding persistent action or it is dead faith!

Persistent Faith Is Relentless, Restless, And Discontented.

From this story, I will leave you with one thought: God will sometimes graciously summon or invite us to struggle with Him so we might avoid apathy or fatalism. And in that point of struggle, we meet with Him and are thus declared men and women of great faith.

Chapter Truths
A PERSISTENT FAITH

1. The Intensity Of Your Adversity Dictates The Strength Of Your Desperation.

2. God Forbid We Walk Away From Our Breakthroughs On Account Of Human Opinion.

3. Persistent Faith Defies The Status Quo.

4. Persistent Faith Is Relentless, Restless, And Discontented.

5. Persistent Faith Arouses Action To The Attainment Of Its Desired End.

Chapter 5
A DESPERATE FAITH

"For she said, 'If I may touch but His clothes, I shall be whole."

Mark 5:28

Imagine a miracle healer coming through a small town; the sick and anyone suffering from *any* condition being healed simply by His command, His word or His touch. Even more marvelous, imagine people healed by simply touching Him. Imagine the sheer pandemonium that would surround such an individual. Well, that was Jesus!

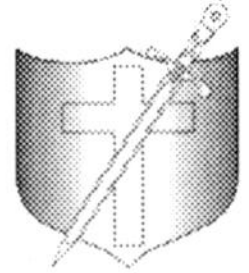

> *"And a certain woman which had an issue of blood twelve years."* (Mark 5:25)

For our purposes, let us call her Leah. Leah had a very big problem: her menstrual period was perpetual.

According to the Law, *"Whenever a woman has her menstrual period, she will be ceremonially unclean for seven days. Anyone who touches her during that time will be unclean until evening. Anything on which the woman lies or sits during the time of her period will be unclean."* (Leviticus 15:19, 20, NLT)

Leah's condition would have completely isolated her. She could not enjoy a hug, a kiss or any kind of physical intimacy even with her own kids. She would have been completely socially shunned.

Deuteronomy says, *"When a man hath taken a wife, and married her, and it come to pass that she find no favour in his eyes, because he hath found some uncleanness in her: then let him write her a bill of divorcement, and give it in her hand, and send her out of his house."* (Deuteronomy 24:1)

Yes, if she was married, her husband would have been allowed, even encouraged by the Law of Moses, to divorce her.

> *"She'd suffered many things of many physicians and had spent all that she had and was nothing bettered."*(Mark 5:26)

Some scholars suggest she might have had some kind of fibroid tumor on her uterus, which modern corrective surgery, such as a hysterectomy, could have fixed. And indeed she tried to get cured by countless physicians. While Mark seems to suggest she was taken advantage of, Luke, perhaps because he was a physician himself, says, *"She had spent all her living upon physicians and could not be healed of ailing."* (Luke 8:43)

Luke basically says it wasn't really the doctor's fault; her ailment was incurable. Regardless, she had a problem which seemed to only get worse with every failed treatment. And since the doctors aren't free, she eventually ran out of money.

Certain Adversities Have No Human Remedies. They Demand Divine Intervention.

Leah was penniless, unclean, rejected, and desperate!

I believe she was a native of Caesarea where Jesus had become very famous. Perhaps she had heard of the miracles; how Jesus had healed the paralytic, the man with the shriveled hand, the centurion's servant, the dead widow's son and many others. Both Mark and Matthew write:

> *"...As many as touched Him were made whole."* (Mark 6:56; Matthew 14:36)

Think about that statement for a minute. *Whoever* touched Jesus was made whole. Wow! Can you imagine the crowds, the chaos, the noise, the desperate cries, the shrieks of joy from those healed, the frustration of those who couldn't get close, the pushing and shoving, the pandemonium?

Even then, imagine Leah wondering, "Since Jesus is coming this way, what if He could cure me? What if Jesus could actually end this vexing nightmare?" And then imagine the discouragement: "Well, how on earth am I ever going to get close enough? With all these people, there is no way He is ever going to see me. And besides, if they even knew I was here, everyone would disperse. They would never let me get close to Him; His disciples, His people, the crowd would probably stone me to death."

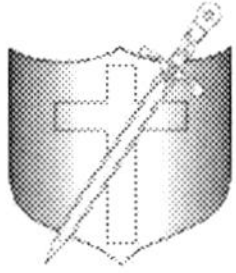

From all three gospel writers, we learn this was a large crowd. One writer called it "a crushing crowd." Another described it as "a pressing crowd." So … lots of folk!

One ancient view stated that if one was a healer, his garments and even his very shadow could heal. This belief might have prompted Leah's next thought, *"If I may touch but His clothes, I shall be whole."*(Mark 5:28)

She probably thought, "Maybe I can get my miracle in a more discreet way. What if I quietly pushed though this crowd and reached for the hem of His garment? What if I could just touch Him?"

Mark 5:27 says,

> *"When she had heard of Jesus, she came in the press behind and she touched His garment."*

Keep in mind that as she squeezed her way through the crushing, pressing, massive crowd, everyone she touched was rendered ritually unclean according to the Law.

We don't know how long it took, but eventually she got close enough to do it. Leah did the riskiest, most amazingly desperate thing: she touched the garments of our Lord Jesus Christ.

Guess what happened?

> *"And straightway the fountain of her blood was dried up; and she felt in her body that she was healed of that plague."* (Mark 5:29)

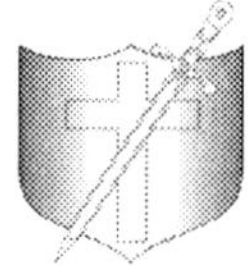

Leah was healed. What? She probably wanted to run; she was probably excited, shocked and certainly dumbfounded. She was likely thinking, "Oh my goodness, it's gone! The terrible nightmare is over. Oh wow! Wow! I'm free. I'm free. But wait; free?

Am I free? Am I really free?"

And then, the thought, "I wonder if Jesus even knows what just happened. Did anyone else see me? I'd better pull back and get to a safe place where I can properly process all this."

Verse 30 says,

> *"And Jesus, immediately knowing in Himself that virtue had gone out of Him, turned Him about in the press, and said, Who touched My clothes?"*

Jesus noticed power had gone out of Him. He knew someone had received a miracle, but yet He asked one of those questions to which He already had an answer. Remember in the book of Genesis when God came in the garden looking for Adam and Eve? He asked, "Adam where art thou?" (Genesis 3:9). Do you really think He didn't know? Or when He asked Cain, after he'd killed his brother, "Where's Abel thy brother?" (Genesis 4:9)

Even When We Believe For It And Fully Expect It; The Manifest Presence Of God Is Bewildering.

Jesus could have simply walked on and thought to Himself, "Wow…someone just got healed." Remember, again, the Bible says, *"As many as touched Him were made whole."* (Matthew 14:36, Mark 6:56)

To me, this implies that stories such as Leah's were probably not uncommon with Jesus. I don't think He stopped every time there was such a healing, do you?

But Jesus has more for Leah.

> *"And His disciples said unto Him, "Thou seest the multitude thronging Thee, and sayest Thou, Who touched Me?"* (Mark 5:31)

In other words,

> *"C'mon Jesus! You can't be serious. Are You really inquiring about a single touch? Seriously? You're literally being manhandled here. We are doing just about all we can do to contain the crowds. We think You should just keep moving so we can make it on time to Jairus' house. Her daughter really needs You right now."*

You would think He would try to give them a reason or try to make them understand, but instead, He says nothing. The Bible says, *"And He looked round about to see her that had done this thing..."* (Mark 5:32)

He just stared into the crowd, waiting for a response.

I'm not sure how long He waited, but meanwhile, something was ensuing:

> *"But the woman fearing and trembling, knowing what was done in her..."* (Mark 5:33a)

Leah probably thought, "Okay. Okay, I thought this was over. I didn't want anyone to even know I was here, but now Jesus is asking. I gotta come clean." She was trembling because of the potential ramifications of her actions. Was she afraid for her life? Was she unsure Jesus would approve of her actions? Would He condemn her? Would she get into trouble with the priests for violating protocol?

As You Celebrate The Miracle, Don't Forget To Read The Message That The Adversity Carried.

Fear gripped her soul.

The Bible says she, *"...came and fell down before Him, and told Him all the truth."* (Mark 5:33c)

Leah laid it all out, probably telling everyone her entire story. Jesus said to her, *"Daughter..."* (Mark 5:34a)

Stop there. "Daughter" implies acceptance. It's an expression of love and concern. Jesus was saying, "I accept you, Leah."

> *"...thy faith has made thee whole."* (Mark 5:34b)

Interesting that Jesus didn't say, "Woman, My incredible, mighty, efficacious, awesome power has healed you." Instead, He said, "Leah, it is your desperate, even ridiculous, I-don't-care-what-this-will-cost-me faith that has done it for you."

Then Jesus said, *"Go in peace and be whole of thy plague..."* (Mark 5:34c)

Jesus accepted her, affirmed her, blessed her and restored her. To put it another way, He said, "Leah, it's okay, you don't have to be afraid. You are completely healed and your illness shall not return. The curse is over!"

Can you imagine Leah walking away completely healed? Can you imagine her walking home to her family and old friends, completely free from this shame? What effectual faith!

Friends, desperate faith moves the Hand of God!

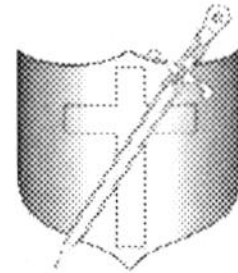

Charlotte was born in Clapham, England on March 18, 1789. She lived a carefree life, gaining popularity as a gifted portrait artist and writer.

As she turned thirty, her health began to fail rapidly. Soon, she became an invalid, and would remain bedridden for the rest of her earthly life.

In 1822, a Swedish evangelist preached Jesus Christ to her, and she gave her life to the Lord. She later wrote:

> *"He knows, and He alone, what it is, day after day, hour after hour, to fight against bodily feelings of almost overpowering weakness, languor and exhaustion, to resolve not to yield to slothfulness, depression and instability, such as the body causes me to long to indulge, but to rise every morning determined to take for my motto, If a man will come after Me, let him deny himself, take up his cross daily, and follow Me."*

Fourteen years later, she penned this timeless song:

Just as I am–without one plea,

But that Thy blood was shed for me,
And that Thou bidst me come to Thee,
O Lamb of God, I come, I come.

Just as I am–and waiting not,
To rid my soul of one dark blot;
To Thee, whose blood can cleanse each spot,
O Lamb of God, I come, I come.

Just as I am–though toss'd about,
With many a conflict, many a doubt,
Fightings and fears within, without,
O Lamb of God, I come, I come!

Just as I am–poor, wretched, blind;
Sight, riches, healing of the mind,
Yea, all I need, in Thee to find,
O Lamb of God, I come, I come.

Just as I am–Thou wilt receive,
Wilt welcome, pardon, cleanse, relieve;
Because Thy promise I believe,
O Lamb of God, I come, I come.
Just as I am–Thy love unknown,
Hath broken every barrier down;
Now, to be Thine, yea, Thine alone,
O Lamb of God, I come, I come.

Just as I am–of that free love,
The breadth, length, depth and height to prove,
Here for a season, then above,
O Land of God, I come![4]

---

[4] Elliot, Charlotte. "Just As I Am, Without One Plea." Richard W. Adams, 1996-2015. Web. 5 Sept. 2015. http://www.hymntime.com/tch/htm/j/u/s/justasam.htm

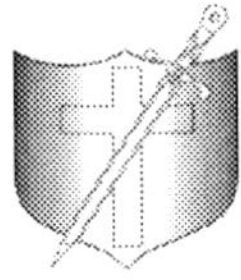

Here is a question I am often asked, especially by learned, analytical, Western audiences: "How come you guys over there in Africa experience all those miracles, while here we hardly see anything?"

Do you know what I say? "We are desperate. We have no Plan B. You guys have it good here: great hospitals, passable roads, good educational system, plenteous job opportunities; yeah, life is good here."

"So what? What's wrong with that?" they ask.

"Well, when Jesus is presented to you, He's merely another 'good thing.' Most of you simply accept Christianity as another good way to live. Going to church on Sunday is good. Not drinking too much is advisable; being faithful to your wife is moral, and so on."

"Now, contrast that with our African experience. Most of us are born in utter impoverishment, live with horrible health conditions, and face the insecurity and uncertainty our daily life brings. There's not a lot of good; in fact for most, it's all bad. When Jesus is presented to us, He is the only good thing. So can you understand why we may treasure our faith a bit more? If you know the nearest doctor is four hours away on foot, through a treacherous, animal infested jungle, those Scriptural promises on healing mean way more to you. We generally don't need to understand why God said what He said, and to whom He said it. We don't really care about theological correctness or exegetical interpretations of God's straightforward promises. We don't reason or argue with Biblical texts. We simply believe. We are desperate and until He touches us, we aren't going anywhere! And guess what? He does touch us!"

When people come to our meetings in Africa, they are desperately hungry for God. It is not uncommon to see someone bringing a dead relative to church. I am currently flying out to California for a Healing Gathering. I can't imagine someone will bring a dead relative to the service tonight to be raised to life by Jesus. People would call the police. But not in Africa—leprosy, AIDS, cancers, demoniacs, and all manner of chronically sick people are brought to Jesus. We have witnessed Jesus do wonders and set all manner of captives free. I have personally witnessed at least nine dead people come back to life, not because God loves us more than our brethren in the West, but because our circumstances have produced within us that crazy, take-no-prisoners, desperate faith.

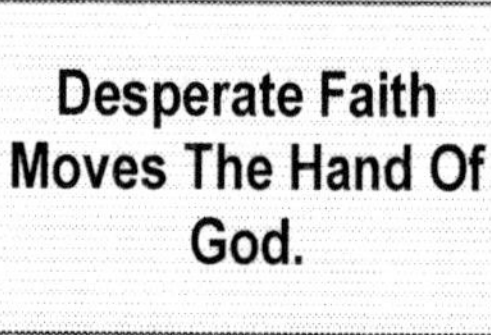
Desperate Faith
Moves The Hand Of
God.

Chapter Truths
A DESPERATE FAITH

1. **Certain Adversities Have No Human Remedies. They Demand Divine Intervention.**

2. **Even When We Believe For It And Fully Expect It; The Manifest Presence Of God Is Always Bewildering.**

3. **As You Celebrate The Miracle, Don't Forget To Read The Message That The Adversity Carried.**

4. **Desperate Faith Moves The Hand Of God.**

Chapter 6
A RECKLESS FAITH

"… Lord, if it be Thou, bid me come unto Thee on the water."

Matthew 14:28

> *"And straightway Jesus constrained His disciples to get into a ship, and to go before Him unto the other side, while He sent the multitudes away."* (Matthew 14:22)

That word "constrained" is the Greek word *anagkazo.* It means to persuade; to compel. Why would Jesus arm-wrestle His disciples to get into a ship? It's because He, essentially, was giving them the easier job. Remember, He was their master. He had been teaching all day, perhaps in the hot sun and would have, by then, been exhausted. The grueling task of dismissing the crowd should have been performed by the apostles, not Jesus. I can imagine the back and forth:

"Guys, you go ahead and I will close the meeting."

"What? No way, Jesus. Please, You go and we'll take care of this."

"No, I insist, you guys go. Let Me dismiss the crowds. Shouldn't take long."

Anagkazo … as their master, Jesus persuaded them—compelled them—and He prevailed.

> *"And when He had sent the multitudes away, He went up into a mountain apart to pray: and when the evening was come, He was there alone. But the ship was now in the midst of the sea, tossed with waves: for the wind was contrary."* (Matthew 14:23-24)

So, there they were, about four miles out in the middle of the Tiberius Sea, when a windstorm began to overtake them. Interestingly, there is no mention of rain, just ferocious wind. The Greek word used here is *enantios,* which means "hostile" and "oppositional". It is worth mentioning that Jesus was on his way to Gadara to deliver a demoniac who had terrorized the entire countryside. The enemy was likely intent on stopping Him. That one miracle would forever impact the entire region.

Isn't it curious that Jesus constrained His disciples to go ahead of Him right into a ferocious windstorm? Think about that for a moment. Jesus Christ sent His beloved disciples into a potentially deadly situation. Here's a question: have you ever followed Christ's instructions, done exactly what you should do and instead of blessings, success, or fulfillment, you encountered disaster? This is one of the most confusing aspects of our walk of faith. We know God is good. We know He thinks good things about us and desires to bestow His blessings upon us, right? We also know that obedience to Him and His Word causes favor to overtake us. So…what's up with these unpredictable windstorms?

Sometimes God Will Lead You Right Into A Savage Storm.

Martha prayed for a husband for years. Supernaturally, she met Tom. Tom is a godly man and everything she ever wanted in a husband. By every definition, Tom is a blessing. But six months into their marriage, Tom developed a freak migraine headache. No matter what he did, the punishing pain only got worse. They decided to get him checked out. Three weeks later, the results were in: Tom had an inoperable tumor on his brain and was given six months to live. WINDSTORM!

Mark and Liz have been praying for a child for twelve years. Since they have tried fertility treatments with no success, they decided to stop all medical remedies and completely trust God for a miracle. One year later, Liz was pregnant; they were thrilled. Julie was born naturally to the sheer delight of her parents, their families and friends. They could not have been more delighted. Three months later, Julie didn't seem responsive to critical stimuli. Further tests revealed a rare brain disorder. They were devastated. WINDSTORM!

What do you do when calamity, setbacks, failure or disaster sideswipes you?

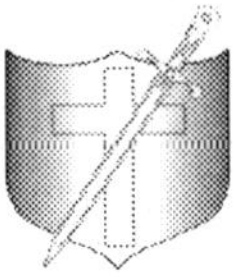

> *"And in the fourth watch of the night Jesus went unto them, walking on the sea."* (Matthew 14:25)

The Jews divided the night into four watches: 6:00 p.m. to 9:00 p.m., 9:00 p.m. to midnight, midnight to 3:00 a.m., and 3:00 a.m. to 6:00 a.m. Jesus would have come walking on that water between 3:00 a.m. and daylight—real early in the morning. This also means they hadn't slept a wink.

> *"And when the disciples saw Him walking on the sea, they were troubled, saying, 'It is a spirit; and they cried out for fear."* (Matthew 14:26)

Please imagine with me for a moment: These guys had struggled all night to keep their boat dry. They had to have been completely wiped out. As hope fades, they see this image of a person walking on the lake. Now, keep in mind that according to Jewish tradition, only God could walk on water. So when they see this figure walking on water, their brains only go to one place: this must be some form of a god or a spirit. Never mind that the figure looks familiar; that in front of them is their beloved master Jesus Christ. Yeah, this is the same Jesus who had turned water into wine, caused an incredible catch of fish, cleansed a leper, healed a paralytic, raised a widow's son from death, raised Jairus' daughter, healed two blind men, and had just miraculously fed thousands of people.

If you were in their shoes, wouldn't you be absolutely relieved to see the same miracle-working Jesus walking right in front of you? Wouldn't you feel a sudden burst of hope and relief? Well, they didn't. You see, their minds could not process the obvious contradiction: Jesus in the midst of a windstorm?

In A Real Windstorm, Jesus Looks Like A Ghost.

You and I do it all the time. Instead of running to Him during our calamitous moments, we instead tend to ask: how can God be here in my pain and my confusion? How can God come to my prison cell? He is supposed to have vindicated me. Why do I feel the glory of God by my hospital bed? He should have prevented me from getting deathly ill in the first place. How is it that I can feel His presence and favor in this messy child custody battle? God should have saved my marriage. Friends, in a real windstorm Jesus looks like a ghost. He doesn't look real because we keep thinking, "This couldn't be God!"

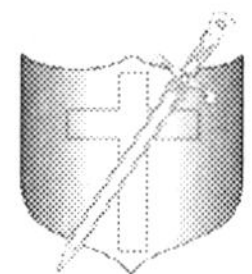

I can't imagine just how long they must have debated, as they struggled to keep the boat dry. What was Jesus doing? Was He still staring at them, smiling at them? He was probably thinking, *Guys, yes, this is Me; take a closer look at My hair, My eyes, My robe.* We can only speculate.

> *"But straightway Jesus spake unto them, saying, 'Be of good cheer; it is I; be not afraid."* (Matthew 14:27)

He was saying, "Yup, it's Me in this mess; it's Me in the midst of this disaster!" To you and me, Jesus says, "Yes, you are losing your home; yes your house is being swept away by the tsunami, but I am with you. Yes, I am aware of this crazy contradiction; in fact, I am in it! It is I—I am here."

> *"And Peter answered Him and said, 'Lord, if it be Thou, bid me come unto Thee on the water."* (Matthew 14:28)

I want you to stop to think about Peter's crazy proposition. Remember, they were struggling to stay afloat, to keep their boat dry. They were barely hanging on; struggling for their lives. They saw what looked like Jesus, but they needed to make sure. Mister Outspoken Peter had an idea:

> *"Jesus, if it's really You doing this cool thing that only a god can do, let me know so I can come join You. I want to come do what You are doing. Indeed, we could possibly perish tonight, but bid me to come to You where I will most certainly perish if it's not You. But if I don't die, then I will know it is You." Does that even make sense? Remember, they did not even know it was really Jesus.*

If that were me, I wouldn't make such a risky proposition. If this were my miracle-performing, wonder-working master right there, I would ask Him to immediately make the storm stop; wouldn't you? That's what most rational humans would do first. Okay, how about a sign in the sky like a big golden star or something? Why not ask Him to prove Himself while you watch? Why ask Jesus to have you risk your own life in order to prove Himself to you?

Faith Is Absolutely Reckless And Completely Irrational.

That was Simon Peter's absolutely reckless faith!

Jesus was probably thinking, "Way to go Peter. You really want to adventure with Me? Okay! Let's do this."

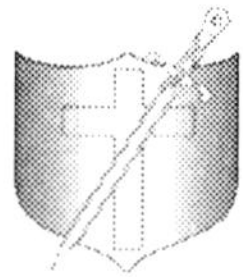

"And He said, 'Come." (Matthew 14:29a)

Can you imagine what his buddies were thinking?

Imagine John, closest friend of Jesus, saying, "Peter! You know how much I love Jesus; you know He and I are really tight, but even I wouldn't do that." Can you imagine analytical Andrew thinking, "Peter! Think, man! We are humans…we can't do that. We sink. You will perish, mate!" Or doubting Thomas saying, "Peter, that form out there sure does look like Jesus, even sounds like Jesus, but I really doubt it is Jesus. I wouldn't risk it, bro." Imagine homeboy Phillip from Caesarea saying, "Hey Peter, if this thing doesn't work out, what should I tell your wife? How do I explain this to your kids?"

I am sure you get the point. I can imagine the murmuring of the disciples on the boat. I don't think they just sat there and watched their buddy do this completely absurd, crazy thing.

Friends, we all have those people whom I call boat-mates. They know your strengths and limitations and sometimes they even deeply care for you. Your business is collapsing, and naturally, you should tighten your spending, maybe not give as much, right? You should stay safe in your boat and focus on keeping it dry. But instead, you want to double your giving, go on a missions trip to Africa or buy weekly groceries for a family in need. That's what I am talking about. Can you imagine the counsel of your boat-mates? "Be wise, man. You are being fanatical. Calm down. You will do more when you have more. You should be saving your money right now."

You've been hurt and bruised and broken, so your boat-mates will advise you to hold back, be careful whom you trust, and so on, but instead, God is drawing you to trust some stranger. In reality, He is saying, "COME! Step out of your boat and do something crazy with me!"

That's what it looks like when you are stepping out of the boat.

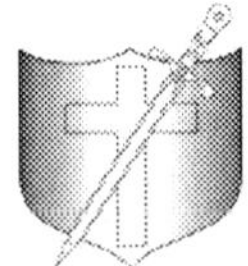

My journey is filled with such invitations.

I remember stepping out to play the drums. No one thought I had it in me. In fact, they told me I didn't have the pedigree of a true drummer. But, thank God I didn't listen. As a result of my obedience, God completely revolutionized praise and worship music throughout our nation. But I was not done…I felt as though God had more.

Your Boatmates Will Rarely Understand Your Divine Invitation To Step Out Of Your Boat.

I started feeling drawn to the keyboards. Completely untrained, my boatmates said drummers couldn't really play modern instruments—they stick to their genre. Thank God I didn't listen. I learned to play the accordion, keyboards, and guitar. I ended up creating new fusions of African pop that drew thousands of young people to Christ. God used us to champion a new musical style which helped usher in a nationwide revival.

I felt God had more.

I felt it was time to sing. My boat-mates said, "Hey, musicians don't sing, y'know! Just keep playing; it's good enough!" Thank God I didn't listen. I learned to sing, and even write songs. My friends and I formed an award-winning ensemble that released five CD's and broke records worldwide.

Still, I felt God had more.

After singing all over the world for seventeen years, I started to feel that familiar pull: "Dennis, get out of the boat. Come walk with Me!" But I was safe. We were very successful. The Lord was telling me I would train leaders around the world. But I hadn't even finished college. My father had passed away a month before I was to enroll in the only university in Uganda. Still, I jumped out of the boat. I became a voracious reader, devouring three books a week. The Lord led me to meet Dr. Douglas Wingate, the president of Life Christian University. God gave me favor with him and he offered to scholarship me through my undergraduate journey. Meanwhile, we were still singing weekly around the world. I would order multiple courses from the university and gobbled up every paragraph of information; I was hungry. I completed my Bachelor's degree, followed by my Master's, and eventually my first Ph.D.—all in record time. My friends would ask, "Dennis, you are safe here, why would you want to think about stepping out there into something you don't even know will work? And do you even know what you really want?" I didn't know why, but something inside my gut was saying *this is the next season of your life and you need to prepare*. I completed my higher education, took a job at a church overseeing a college startup program. The International College of Excellence would explode, spawning twenty-two extension campuses in eight countries.

I felt God had more.

No One Is Ever Really Sure They Can Walk On Water Before They Actually Step Out Of The Boat.

I resigned from the school and launched a global missionary organization called Eagle's Wings International. And the rest, as they say, is history. I have since authored over a dozen books, pastored a local congregation in Chicago, and ministered to millions of people in seventy countries.

As the Lord draws me out once again, I am now cautious of the counsel of my boat-mates. I know sometimes the invitation seems too crazy, and a mere, "Dennis, are you sure?" could be enough to cause me to choose safety. You see, in reality, I am never really sure—I am not sure it is really Jesus walking on that water. Here's a secret: *no one* really ever is.

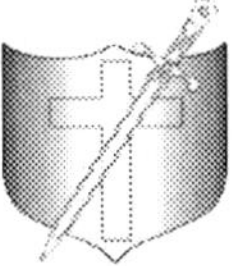

> *"And when Peter was come down out of the ship, he walked on the water, to go to Jesus."* (Matthew 14:29b)

Peter did it! He actually walked on water, something humans cannot do. I know most of us remember this story from Peter's failure, but the bigger deal here is: *he walked on the water to go to Jesus*. Can we give the guy some serious kudos for that?

> *"But when he saw the wind boisterous, he was afraid; and beginning to sink, he cried, saying, 'Lord, save me.'"* (Verse 30)

You Walk On Water Because Of Your Unswerving Focus On Jesus.

Can one really see wind? Whether Peter literally did, or whether he saw its effects, he freaked out. Question: did the wind suddenly appear? Did it just suddenly get super-windy? No. The wind was always there. Peter began walking on the water because he had his eyes transfixed on Jesus. He was doing well until he looked at what had always been there: he looked at the crazy, pre-existing circumstance—the windstorm—and began to sink.

> *"And immediately Jesus stretched forth His hand, and caught him, and said unto him, O thou of little faith, wherefore didst thou doubt?"* (Verse 31)

Jesus stretched forth His hand and caught Peter, basically saying to him, "Oh, Peter, you were doing so well, what happened?" When I first read this, I thought, *Man, Jesus, why not give the guy a break? Aren't You being a little hard on Your buddy Peter?* But Jesus was teaching Peter a priceless lesson. "Peter, you might be able to do that doubting thing while over there on the boat, but once you stepped out, you lost that luxury. Over here, once you take your eyes off of Me you will certainly perish."

Once you begin walking on water—after you make the move out of safety and familiarity—you don't have the luxury of doubt. You simply cannot afford to look at your circumstances.

It is worth mentioning that when Peter looked at his circumstances, he was only being natural. He was acting like a normal, logical human being. When we hear wind, we naturally panic and get distracted. But, what this text tells me is, after we make the decision to walk by faith, we cannot walk by sight any longer. While doubt on the boat is precarious, on the water it becomes fatal.

After You Step Out Of The Boat, You Cannot Afford The Luxury Of Doubt.

Jojo stepped away from his stable, decades-long career to start his own business. For the first couple of years it was touch-and-go. He never knew how his bills were paid, but somehow he was always in the black. Vendors were paid on time and God was supernaturally blessing his young business. Suddenly, the housing market crashed and an economic depression ensued. He saw the boisterous wind and began to freak out. Questions began to swarm in his mind:

"How am I surviving?"

"How am I paying all these bills?"

"What if I can't afford to keep this going?"

"What if I lose all my customers?"

Jojo is looking away from Jesus and unless he immediately corrects, his fears will surely come to pass.

> *"And when they were come into the ship, the wind ceased. Then they that were in the ship came and worshipped Him, saying, Of a truth Thou art the Son of God."* (Verse 32, 33)

Notice the Bible doesn't say Peter jumped on Jesus' back. The 100% human Peter actually walked back to the boat, with Jesus, on the water! Can you imagine the whispers of his boat-mates as they helped him back into the boat? Astonishment. Admiration. Maybe some envy.

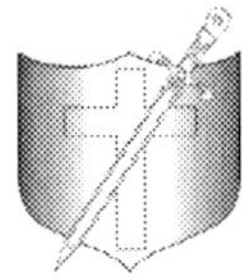

Storms will come through transitions, intrusions, internal uprisings, relationship crashes, growth plateaus, and disillusionment. Sometimes your church becomes stifling when things that used to matter no longer do. Is your life curled up into a question mark? You might be in a storm. Jesus is with you; listen for His instruction to step out of your ship.

You're in the boat, where things are:

- Familiar
- Safe
- Normal
- Predictable
- Reasonable

Step out into the water, where it's:

- Unfamiliar
- Unsafe
- Dangerous
- Disruptive
- Unpredictable

- Unreasonable

You say, "Dennis I am in a really bad situation right now. I need courage to step out of the boat. I am freaked out."

Pray this with me:

> "*Father, I pray You would stir up inside me that reckless faith to completely step out of this boat, and to remain transfixed upon You as I walk upon these turbulent waters to the place of Your assignment. In Jesus' name! Amen.*"

You Will Never Do Anything Great For God Until You Step Out Of Your Boat.

Chapter Truths
A RECKLESS FAITH

1. **Sometimes God Will Lead You Right Into A Savage Storm.**

2. **In A Real Windstorm, Jesus Looks Like A Ghost.**

3. **Faith Is Absolutely Reckless And Completely Irrational.**

4. **Your Boatmates Will Rarely Understand Your Divine Invitation To Step Out Of Your Boat.**

5. **No One Is Ever Really Sure They Can Walk On Water Before They Actually Step Out Of The Boat.**

6. **You Walk On Water Because Of Your Unswerving Focus On Jesus.**

7. **After You Step Out Of The Boat, You Cannot Afford The Luxury Of Doubt.**

8. **You Will Never Do Anything Great For God Until You Step Out Of Your Boat.**

Chapter 7
A COSTLY FAITH

"Sell everything you have and give to the poor, and you will have treasure in heaven. Then come, follow Me."

Luke 18:22 (NIV)

It is almost the end of Jesus' public ministry. He was very popular; immensely popular in fact. To put it in modern terms, Jesus was totally famous. He was *IT*! If you hadn't heard of Him, you just hadn't been around town; or perhaps you'd been isolated from all human interaction. Everyone, even the kids, knew who He was.

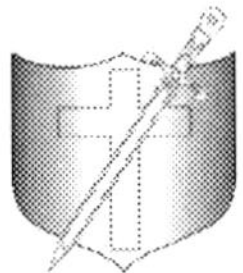

> *"As Jesus started on His way, a certain ruler ran up to Him and fell on his knees before Him."* (Mark 10:17, NIV)

The Greek word for "ruler" here is *archon*, which means *an authority, an official, a leader in the synagogue, or a member of the ruling Jewish council, the Sanhedrin.*

Matthew's gospel describes this man as a young man, *nianiskos* in the Greek. This word indicates he might have been between the age of twenty-four and forty.

Luke later refers to him as very great, or a man of great wealth. The Greek word used there for "wealth" is the word *pluosios*, which means *one who has an abundance of earthly possessions.*

So, Jesus is approached by a young, energetic, rich man of high societal pedigree. He falls down before Him and pleads with intense longing. You can imagine what a stir this would have caused. Remember; in this culture rich people looked noticeably well off. They dressed ornately, were groomed handsomely, and even smelled different.

Rich Or Poor, We All Hunger For Living Water In Much The Same Way.

I have met many a very wealthy man who looked anything but rich. There is a growing trend these days in some Western countries to dress down and look ordinary; it's supposed to be cool. I remember going to dinner with a wealthy man who also happened to be very generous. The waitress was rude to us; she didn't care to serve us with excellence. I bet she wished she'd gotten a different table. All the while I thought, *Lady, you better get yourself together because if you do your job well with this table, you are about to be very blessed! This man here could buy this whole building!* Our waitress was distracted by the simple jeans and T-shirt look.

Well, not back then. When one was wealthy, everyone could see it. In fact, they wanted everyone to know.

This man had a burning question. Humble, earnest, and broken he asked, *"...What must I do to inherit eternal life?"* (Luke 18:18b)

That was a rather intelligent question. First of all, it shows he believed in eternal life, indicating he was probably one of the Pharisees, the largest religious sect to believe in life after death.

His question can be paraphrased this way: "Jesus, I need the combination or formula for the "gate" to Eternal Life. Please tell me what I need to do to get in."

Jesus looked at him and said, *"You know the commandments: 'You shall not commit adultery, you shall not murder, you shall not steal, you shall not give false testimony, honor your father and mother.'"* (Luke 18:20, NIV)

I can imagine as Jesus went down the list, this devout, learned man was probably smiling. I can imagine him thinking, "Check, Check" after each commandment. He had to respond; he must let Jesus know just how good he has been; just how devout he is. He said, *"All these I have kept since I was a boy, he said."* (Verse 21)

Essentially, he was saying, "Jesus, I've got it. I already got it all down. Remember, I am *archon*. I keep the law—all of it. I am a devout man, and have been at this—keeping the Law of Moses—since I was a kid!"

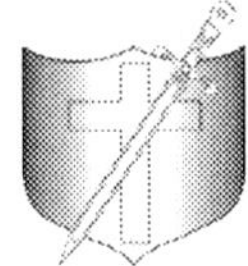

Can you imagine the stares from the audience?

"What is Jesus going to say next? This guy just told Him His prescription is not enough."

Instead of debating him... *"...Jesus, beholding him, loved him..."* (Mark 10:21)

He had compassion upon him, and then said to him, *"You still lack one thing."*

He felt compassion for him, as He pointed out his oversight and then challenged him to do a most courageous thing: *"Sell everything you have and give it to the poor and you will have treasure in heaven."* (Luke 18:22, NIV)

In other words he said, "Okay, you rich and powerful, classy young leader, here is my prescription for your hunger: G*o sell all your stuff. Just get rid of it.*" Jesus knew very well that by giving away his stuff, he would lose his:

- Wealth
- Power
- Status
- Security
- Influence
- Pedigree
- Identity
- VERY SELF!

The Rich Young Ruler Had A "Knowing Faith," Which Left Him Thirsty!

Although he had kept all God's laws, he still had himself. His money gave him an identity that had suffocated his spiritual life.

For years, I thought this story meant Jesus was anti-money. I thought He wanted all of us to be empty of all earthly possessions and to take vows of poverty. That's not true.

Throughout the Gospels, we see Jesus encountering wealthy people like Mary, Simon the Pharisee, Joseph of Aramathea, Nicodemus, Zachaeus, Joanna, Susanna and many others. He never said, "Okay, rich Simon, now that you have hosted Me in your lovely home, I want you to give it all away." Or to Zacchaeus who offered to give four times back to anyone he has wronged, "No buddy, I want it all gone. This money is evil!" He didn't. Without the wealth and power of Joseph and Nicodemus, Jesus' body would have not been preserved for His immaculate resurrection.

My aim is not to esteem wealth. On the contrary, being wealthy can be a problem. Jesus goes so far as to say it is impossible for the rich to enter the Kingdom of God, except by a miracle (Matthew 19:24). The rich have to contend with vanity, ambition, and what I call "more-ness!" The poor are actually free from certain *wants*! An African teenager has no expectation for a car when he turns eighteen; he just hopes he'll still be alive. Poor people are generally aware of their limitations and helplessness. They only have what they *must* have.

I was born and raised in a very poor country; the thirteenth poorest country in the world at the time. I know firsthand how agonizing the pangs of poverty really are. Suffice it to say, living in poverty isn't synonymous with righteousness. I've also seen very mean, greedy, and selfish poor people. But Jesus says, "Blessed be the poor, for yours is the Kingdom of God." (Luke 6:20) He in fact comes to preach the Gospel to the poor. (Luke 4:18)

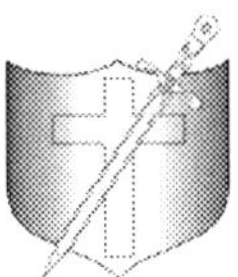

Thus, Jesus had a very simple prescription for this rich young ruler: "Give away your stuff; your safety net, your status and altitude, your prominence and class, and instead you will have Me. You want the Kingdom of God? Lose yourself. Give yourself away! But that's not all ... *"And take up your cross and follow Me."* (Luke 9:23)

Jesus Is Not Anti-Money. He Simply Wants Us To Love Him More.

The proposition Jesus presented is painfully inconvenient. He suggests an exchange: Your wealth for Him, your identity for His! This young ruler was offered a seat at Jesus' table. Amazing!

The Bible says, *"When he heard this, he became very sorrowful for he was VERY rich."* (Luke 18:23, emphasis)

He just couldn't give it up. It's not that he had stuff; so much as stuff had *him*. He walked away, never inheriting the Kingdom of God.

Can you imagine the following day? Twice daily, this devout Jew would have had to recite what they call the *Shema,* out of Deuteronomy 6:4-5. Part of it says, *"Hear O Israel: The Lord our God, the Lord is one. Love the Lord your God with all your heart and with all your soul and with all your strength."* (NIV)

It goes on to read: *"You shall have no other gods before Me."*

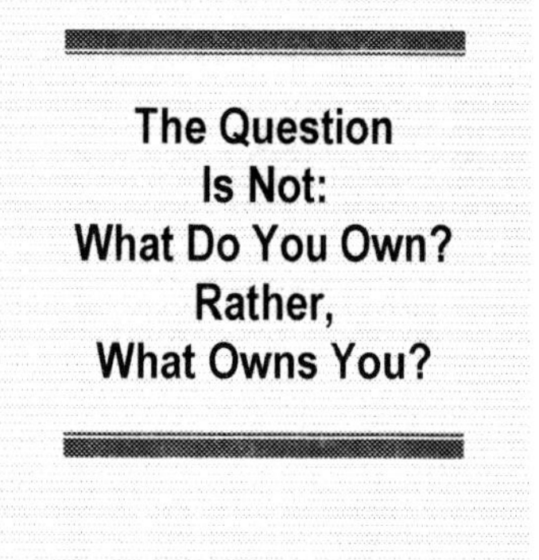

The Question
Is Not:
What Do You Own?
Rather,
What Owns You?

How do you do that, knowing just yesterday Jesus told you exactly what it would take for you to inherit the Kingdom of heaven, but instead you chose to walk away because your money, power or status was more important? That your membership in the Sanhedrin was more important to you than a spot at the table with the Son of David! Was he invited to become another one of the disciples? Maybe, but he knew he was given a seat at the table.

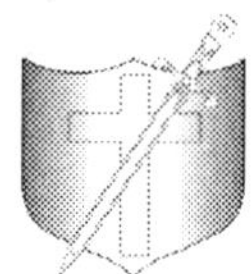

What owns you? What has possession of your heart?

For this young man it was money.

For the lonely and divorced Sarah, it was her boyfriend. "I really want to be a Christian, but my boyfriend isn't ready. We live together. I just can't live without him. I just can't."

Zuma said, "Yeah, but I've got this good job. Problem is, I have to constantly lie to my customers. Becoming a Christian means I'd have to change jobs. Can't, mate! I have to survive."

Jamal says, "I want to get closer to Jesus, but I am not ready to give up my social life. My buddies and I, we get drunk every weekend, have wild parties and forget our troubles. If I stop drinking, I'll lose my friends. We have known each other since we were kids."

My friend, maybe you know God's commands. Maybe you know how to do church, sing the songs, and even serve in your local community. Maybe you have a cosmetic Christianity—you do all the right things, but your heart isn't completely given to God. As you read this, Jesus is proposing a great exchange: "Give Me your stuff, your identity, your status, and I'll give you My life, my identity, and eternal life."

Jesus Proposes This Great Exchange: Lose It All So You Can Gain Eternal Life.

All over the world, there seems to be a growing school of thought in Christendom that espouses a convenient Christianity. This is a false gospel. Indeed, Jesus paid it all, but He also says, *"...If any man would come after Me, let him deny himself, and take up his cross daily, and follow Me."* (Luke 9:23, ASV)

That culture knew exactly what He meant. A cross was never a good thing. It meant shame, ridicule, and the bottom of the bottom!

Authentic faith is costly. Indeed, it is given freely, but there is an exchange. Will you give yourself away?

Chapter Truths
A COSTLY FAITH

1. **Rich Or Poor, We All Hunger For Living Water In Much The Same Way.**

2. **The Rich Young Ruler Had A "Knowing Faith," Which Left Him Thirsty!**

3. **Jesus Is Not Anti-Money. He Simply Wants Us To Love Him More!**

4. **The Question Is Not: What Do You Own? Rather, What Owns You?**

5. **Jesus Proposes This Great Exchange: Lose It All So You Can Gain Eternal Life.**

Chapter 8
A PRECIOUS FAITH

"There came unto Him a woman having an alabaster box of very precious ointment, and poured it on His head."

Matthew 26:7

> *"And a whole multitude sought to touch Him: for there went virtue out of Him, and healed them all."* (Luke 6:19)

Can you imagine the throngs of sick, desperate people, people at the end of their rope, yearning for a touch, a word, a glance from Him? There were also those adoring fans who would hang on to every word from his lips. Don't forget the critics looking for a way to trap him; the curious hearts in search of answers. And what about the grateful multitudes who had been touched by Him? What an amazing human being!

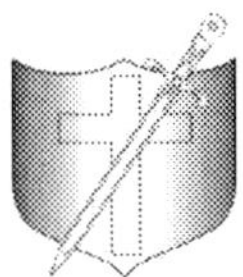

"Behold a woman in this city which was a sinner ..."

How did they know? Perhaps she was dressed like one. Maybe they knew her. I grew up in a small village community much like this where everyone knew pretty much what everyone else was into. If a young girl became pregnant, everyone knew it and they all called her shameful.

> *"... when she knew that Jesus sat at meat in the Pharisee's house ..."*

When she heard Jesus was having dinner at this rich Pharisee's house, she, "*... brought an alabaster of ointment.*" (Luke 7:37)

Jesus must have really been exhausted from the grind of His ministry and was relaxing, just hanging out at this Pharisee's home. I can imagine there was probably some security to control access to the house. We can also safely assume this private banquet was an invitation-only event with the host's more prominent friends.

I can imagine this woman coming in, definitely uninvited. She looked wrong, indelicate, and loose; she clearly didn't belong. There were probably whispers of disbelief and disgust; I can almost hear them ask, "Who does she think she is, coming here uninvited?"

She ignored them.

Dinner tables were normally low to the ground and without chairs. They would lay down with their feet exposed at their side. Suffice it to say, feet were the dirtiest part of the body due to all the dust in that dry desert area.

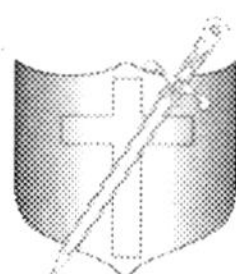

She had a box made out of a white, marble-like substance called alabaster. Alabaster boxes typically had ointment, oils, or perfume in them and were sealed with wax to keep the contents pure and unspoiled, and to prevent them from spilling out. This was a very costly box!

> *"She stood at His feet behind Him, she's weeping and began to wash His feet and did wipe them with the hairs of her head, and kissed His feet, and anointed them with the ointment."* (Luke 7:38)

Why was she weeping? Was she convicted? Perhaps she was feeling like: *I know you people are judging me, but I don't really care. I am in front of the kindest Man to ever walk the earth and I really need to worship Him right now*. This uninvited, sinful woman was crying and embarrassing everyone with her uncomfortable display of affection for the Chief Guest.

Water was customarily provided before one entered a house, to help them wash off the desert dust. It's interesting to note that only slaves washed other's feet. This woman took the posture of a slave, giving no consideration to cultural norms. Can you imagine how many tears it must have taken to wash the desert dust off of Jesus' feet? She had no napkin, and no hand-cloth to dry them; instead, she used her hair.

In that culture, hair represented dignity. In fact, decent women covered their hair. It was scandalous to have it out, let alone to wash another's feet with it. But she was a sinner.

Another norm was women didn't touch men who were not their husbands. But again, she was a sinner.

She kissed Jesus' feet after they were clean and then proceeded to break her expensive alabaster box. The room must have filled with fragrance. This must have raised eyebrows, and most definitely infuriated the host and his guests.

People Will Always Have An Opinion About Your Sacrifice.

They had to say something: *"This Man if He were a prophet would have known who and what manner of woman this is that touches Him for she is a sinner."* (Luke 7:39b)

In other words: "If this guy is really legit; if this Jesus is really who they say He is or who He is professing to be, He should know this is not a decent woman; that this woman is not worthy of His attention or this kind of access." They thought Jesus was too special for her. She was too soiled to get that close to an esteemed teacher of Jesus' caliber.

Clearly, they had a strong opinion about her sacrifice, and they made it known.

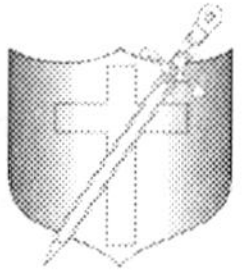

Jesus responded with a story:

> *"There was a certain creditor, which had two debtors: the one owed five hundred pence, and the other fifty. And when they had nothing to pay, he frankly forgave them both. Tell me therefore, which of them will love him most?"* (Luke 7:41-42)

Simon Peter, often the quickest responding disciple, said, *"The one who was forgiven the most."*

Jesus said, *"Do you see this woman? I entered into your house and you gave Me no water for My feet."* (Verse 44a)

This was a courtesy especially befitting a guest of this stature. He was saying, "You did not do, for Me, what is customary. I am seated here for dinner and My feet are dirty." This must have embarrassed His hosts, but that was not His intention. He was after something much bigger.

> *"But she hath washed My feet with tears, and wiped them with the hairs of her head. Thou gavest Me no kiss: but this woman since the time I came in hath not ceased to kiss My feet. My head with oil thou didst not anoint: but this woman hath anointed My feet with ointment."* (Verse 44b-46)

He was saying this woman had done more for Him than anyone there; just leave her be, leave her alone.

Then He brings it home: *"Wherefore I say unto thee, Her sins, which are many, are forgiven; for she loved Me much: but whom little is forgiven, the same loveth little."* (Verse 47)

Her grand gesture was because of her faith; she had a lot to be thankful for.

Only You Know What It Will Cost You To Break Your Box of Alabaster.

I see such faith around the world in our travels; men and women who have been delivered from unspeakable molestation, abuse or chronic illnesses. You can't get the smile off their faces; you can't stop them from singing out loud, or from throwing their hands in the air. You can't stop them from giving, loving, or sharing their story with others. You cannot stop them from breaking open their alabaster boxes upon the feet of their Lord.

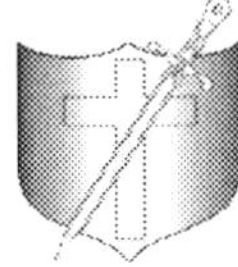

Let me give you three take-away lessons from this story:

1. Everyone has a box. Everyone has something that is precious to them. Only you know the cost, the value of your oil or the ointment in your box. Is it your boyfriend, your wife, your job, your popularity, your reputation, or your friends? Only you know.

2. Your sacrifice will draw attention. Once you take that box and break it upon the feet of Jesus, people are going to say: "He's given up his girlfriend?" "She's given up her job?" People will have an opinion about your sacrifice—always! Which brings us to the next lesson …

3. The world will despise your sacrifice. People aren't going to think how cool it is that you've given up your six-figure income to move to Africa and serve that needy village community. I have seen celebrities who get saved, make the news cycle and then endure a barrage of attacks for their faith. If you are looking for pats on the back, you will never step out into what God has for you.

There Is Something Precious That You Must Break Before The Lord.

The story doesn't end there. Jesus said to the woman, *"Thy faith hath saved thee; go in peace."* (Verse 50)

That's what we are talking about in this chapter. The faith to give what's precious!

I end this chapter with this question: what is that precious something you need to break before the Lord?

Chapter Truths
A PRECIOUS FAITH

1. **Everyone Has A Story.**

2. **People Will Always Have An Opinion About Your Sacrifice.**

3. **Only You Know What It Will Cost You To Break Your Box Of Alabaster.**

4. **There Is Something Precious That You Must Break Before The Lord.**

Chapter 9
A SHOUTING FAITH

"...but he cried the more a great deal, Thou son of David, have mercy on me."

Mark 10:48b

> *"And they came to Jericho: and as He went out of Jericho with His disciples and a great number of people, blind Bartimaeus, the son of Timaeus, sat by the highway side begging."* (Mark 10:46)

A very famous Jesus with his rather big entourage was passing through town. He was no stranger to the community—He had grown up there; they knew Him, and His family. Suddenly, He was a huge phenomenon: He touches sick people and they recover. He speaks to demons and they flee. In some instances, even those who touch Him are made well. Can you imagine the chaos that must have followed Him?

"Jesus, me too! Touch me please!"

"Over here, Jesus. My child is dying!"

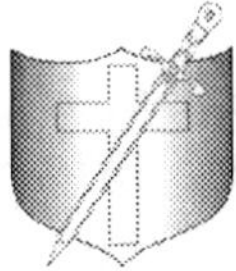

There sat a blind man by the roadside named Bartimaeus. He was the son of Timaeus, who some scholars believe was also blind, suggesting generational blindness. If so, Bartimaeus must have feared his own children would perhaps also suffer blindness.

Like all blind people he lived a dark life, having never seen the sun, the sky, a tree, water, skin, or any colors. He may have felt their texture, but he didn't know what green leaves looked like. He couldn't fathom the visual difference between rough and smooth. He clearly had a desperate need!

There Is Adversity That You Bring Upon Yourself; But Much More Stinging Is The Kind That Is Brought Upon You.

Bartimaeus would naturally pick a busy spot on the roadside, on this busiest weekend of the year: Passover. He would want to collect as much money as possible. I can almost hear him say,

"Help, I'm blind! Alms for the blind!"

> *"And when he heard that it was Jesus of Nazareth..."* (Mark 10:47a)

Yes, *that* Jesus of Nazareth, the famous carpenter's son everyone was talking about! This famed miracle worker's amazing works would have aroused some vivid fantasies for blind Bartimaeus. Imagine his internal dialogue: *If Jesus could miraculously feed thousands, and heal all manner of illnesses, including leprosy, surely He could cure me. But how do I get to see Him? Who will take me to Him? Does anyone know where He is going to be?*

But right here, his opportunity is finally coming down the street. *I can't believe Jesus is coming down this way.* I can imagine him beginning to hope that maybe this was his day. Imagine him thinking: *There is no way I am going to let this opportunity pass me by. This is not going to be just another day for this blind man. I just need to get His attention.*

The Bible says, *"...he began to cry out, and say, Jesus, Thou Son of David, have mercy on me,"* (Mark 10:47b)

Now, this is interesting to me because the Bible says that while he heard it was Jesus of Nazareth coming, Bartimaeus called Him by an entirely different title: *Son of David.* That was the title reserved for the soon-coming Messiah. Everyone knew it. There would only be one Son of David. By Bartimaeus addressing Jesus as Son of David, he is saying several things:

1. Jesus, you are not just a fellow countryman. I don't see You as one of us. You are way more than that!
2. I see You as timeless, the Son of David, as God, the God-man. I see You as You are supposed to be seen and I declare it to everyone.
3. As Son of David, nothing is impossible for You. You can do anything.

Well, even so, Jesus was not moved by his shout. You see, shouts of this nature were commonplace around Jesus the healer. Remember, He could heal *all* manner of illnesses.

"My daughter is sick."

"I am in pain."

"My uncle is dying."

As passionate as it might have been, Bartimaeus' shout was simply a shout of need. This is what I call the *first shout*!

In our meetings around the world, I often ask for a show of hands of those with a need. Almost everyone raises their hand. It's hard to be completely need-free in this fallen world, right? If it isn't your health, then it's your kids; if not your business, it's your marriage. We all agree: life is brutal! But merely having a need is not enough to get God's attention. Not that He doesn't care, but just because you have a need doesn't warrant His intervention. You are not special because you shout, "Ouch!"

Merely Having A Need Doesn't Move The Hand Of God!

To the religious hierarchy, Bartimaeus' cry was almost blasphemous. The last thing they needed was someone screaming such a profound endorsement concerning Jesus. In fact, I believe some of them were involved in what happened next. Verse 48 says, *"Many charged him that he should hold his peace."*

So, in addition to his failure to get the attention of Jesus, now the mean crowd gave him some choice counsel: "Shut up!"

He was rejected.

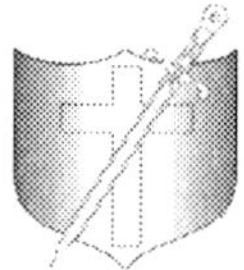

Perhaps if Bartimaeus could see, he might have appreciated the impracticality of his quest. He might have felt too embarrassed to cause such disruption. He would have heeded the counsel of the crowd and faded back to his smallness; his blind corner.

But his condition provided an opportunity. He didn't see the challenge they saw. Bartimaeus had a decision to make: to listen to the "seeing" people, or to hang on to his condition and maybe die blind. He knew they didn't know what it was like to live in perpetual darkness. They had an opinion over something they completely didn't understand and, thus, they would never understand his decision. They didn't know he could not afford to keep quiet. Was it the thought of having to look for another place to beg for alms tomorrow? Was it the longing to finally look upon the faces of his family or friends? Whatever it was, he didn't care about appeasement. He had a burning need, and this was his moment. He dare not let it pass him by.

The Crowd Always Has An Opinion About Your Passion; They Don't Know Your Pain.

Verse 48 says,

> *"...but he cried the more a great deal, 'Thou son of David, have mercy on me.'"*

This is what we call the *desperate shout*. It's not a mere "*ouch*", but a defiance of the status quo. *Jesus, I've got to have You touch me or else*. I call it the *I-don't-care-what-y'all-think* kind of shout. Or, the *y'all-don't-know-what-I'm-going-through* shout. It's not dignified, civil or neat. It's loud, messy, and desperate. It's unpopular, it's uncomfortable and, again, desperate!

> *"And Jesus stood still..."* (Verse 49a)

Yes, this shout gets His attention. He stands still! You only shout again, my friends, because you cannot afford to be quiet.

Sometimes, I get to arrive early at speaking engagements and hang out at the back of the sanctuary before service begins. And I see him. With the band rehearsing and the deacons preparing, he is on his knees, tears rolling down his cheeks, crying to Jesus! As soon as the doors open, he rushes all the way to the front row.

One Of The Greatest Freedoms You Must Seek Is The Freedom From Human Opinion.

The worship begins and he's singing louder than everyone else. He dances harder than anyone on his row, sweating profusely. Then I glance at the folks next to him. You can almost hear them say: *Shhh! Calm yourself down, buddy. You don't have to shout as loud or dance as hard. You bother us when you jump so high into our space. Excuse us; you are too excited for our comfort*.

Sounds like the crowd, doesn't it? But he doesn't care. As I preach, he is the loudest, shouting "Amen!" and getting up on his feet every few minutes.

I watch him at the end of the service as the ushers clear the sanctuary. He is still there quietly rocking back and forth, crying to the Lord. The brother is blind. He cares not for us, the "seeing" people! He needs a miracle from Jesus, and won't leave until He gets His touch!

Jesus Always Wants To Be Chosen.

Jesus said, *"If any man come to Me, and hate not his father, and mother, and wife, and children, and brethren, and sisters, yea, and his own life also, he cannot be My disciple."* (Luke 14:26)

That word "hate" is the Greek word *miseo*, which means to love less. This verse could read, "If any man doesn't love Me more than his father, mother, wife, kids, brothers and sisters, and his own life, he can't be My disciple."

Further ahead in verse 33, He says, *"So likewise, whosoever he be of you that forsaketh not all that he hath, he cannot be My disciple."*

The word right there, "forsake," is the Greek word *apotasso,* which means to separate from, or bid farewell.

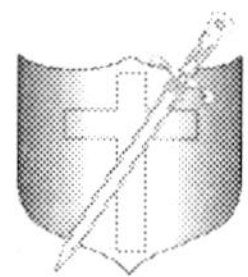

Continuing in Mark 10:49, the Bible says, *"...and commanded him to be called. And they call the blind man, saying unto him, 'Be of good comfort, rise: He calleth thee."*

Whether this is a different crowd that actually roots for Bartimaeus, or the same one who told him to shut up, we learn one big lesson: we cannot trust the crowd. Beware of the "seeing people!" They don't know what it's like to be blind. They don't know what it's like to live in perpetual darkness. They don't know your pain; they don't understand your burden. And how could they? They will never understand how you can't allow such an opportunity like this to pass you by.

Verse 50 says, *"And he, casting away his garment, rose, and came to Jesus."*

Think about this: Bartimaeus' garment was perhaps his most valuable possession. Those garments were given to blind people by the priests to identify them as blind and to authorize them to gather alms.

Be Wary Of Those Dithering "Seeing People". Every Season Has Them!

The word "casting" here is the Greek word *apoballo*, meaning *jerked off, tear free, throw way, or discard*. It gives the picture of a tight, restrictive garment. Bartimaeus would have been tightly clad in his garment and when Jesus says come, he literally yanks away his identity and his source of livelihood, or provision, *before* he is healed. Bartimaeus was a man of faith. He reckoned, *because Jesus said come, I'm never going to be blind again. My healing awaits me, and I don't have to see it yet to believe I am never going to need this raiment again!* Almost reckless, right? Well, when is real faith ever reasonable?

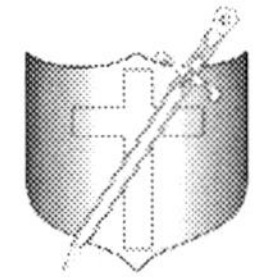

Bartimaeus is brought to Jesus, probably staggering, being held by hand. Then Jesus asked him one of the most ridiculous questions:

"What wilt thou that I should do unto thee?" (Verse 51b)

I'm thinking, isn't it obvious Jesus? Didn't you call him knowing he was blind? Of course He did. Then why ask? Jesus wants us to be clear with our needs. We do prayer lines in many countries throughout the world. The question is often asked, "Hey, what do you want God to do for you?" Some people will say, "Oh, well, whatever God wants," or, "God knows; you just pray."

I am thinking that's a pious-sounding, religiously-correct answer but it's the wrong answer. Bartimaeus could have said, "Well Jesus, You know, You called me out, didn't You?" Instead, he said in verse 51, "*...Lord that I might receive my sight.*"

Jesus said to him: *"Go thy way; thy faith hath made thee whole. And immediately he received his sight, and followed Jesus in the way."*

Bartimaeus received his sight, not because Jesus is powerful or super-anointed. Although He could have, Jesus didn't say, "Go your way, My power has healed you," or, "Go your way, I have made you whole." Instead, He said to him, "You are healed because of your desperate, crazy, reckless, shouting faith. This shout of faith has made you whole." He immediately received his sight, but the story doesn't end there; he received his sight and followed Jesus.

In conclusion, let's list seven lessons from this incredible story.

Bartimaeus:

1. Was open about his condition
2. Believed Jesus the Messiah
3. Persisted in spite of the crowd
4. Answered Jesus' call.
5. Stripped himself of his identity
6. Pleaded for mercy
7. Followed Jesus

Every season has challenges; and every season brings a crowd who will often say to us:

"No you can't!"

"Tone it down!"

"You don't have to go overboard with your passion!"

They don't have to be critics or haters. They could be family, even well-meaning friends who wish to offer advice. Do not give ear to them. Focus on Jesus. Find your second shout of faith!

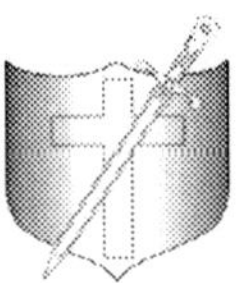

At six weeks old, Fanny Crosby caught a cold, and developed an eye inflammation that destroyed her optic nerves, permanently blinding her. She ran to God. By age ten, she had memorized five chapters of the Bible! By age fifteen, she had memorized Genesis, Exodus, Leviticus, Numbers, Deuteronomy, several Psalms, Proverbs, Song of Solomon, Matthew, Mark, Luke and John. She would play the organ, harp, piano and the guitar. She wrote more than 9,000 songs with over 100 million copies of her songs printed. [5]

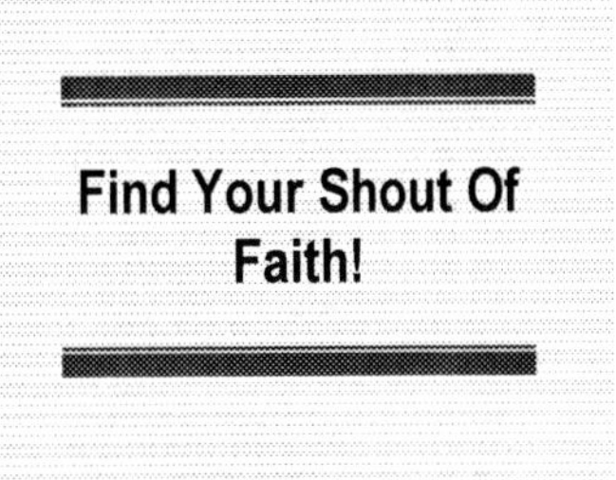
Find Your Shout Of
Faith!

She wrote this timeless hymn:

Pass me not, O gentle Savior,
Hear my humble cry;
While on others Thou art calling,
Do not pass me by.

Chorus:
Savior, Savior,
Hear my humble cry;
While on others Thou art calling
Do not pass me by

---

[5] Crosby, Fanny. *Christianity Today*. 2015 http://www.christianitytoday.com/ch/131christians/poets/crosby.html 5 Sept 2015

Let me at Thy throne of mercy
Find a sweet relief;
Kneeling there in deep contrition,
Help my unbelief.
(Chorus)

Trusting only in Thy merit,
Would I seek Thy face;
Heal my wounded, broken spirit,
Save me by Thy grace.
(Chorus)

Thou the spring of all my comfort,
More than life to me;
Whom have I on earth beside Thee?
Whom in heaven but Thee?

(Chorus)[6]

[6] Crosby, Fannie. "*Pass Me Not, O Gentle Savior.*" http://www.cyberhymnal.org/htm/p/a/passment.htm 5 Sept 2015

Chapter Truths
A SHOUTING FAITH

1. **There Is Adversity That You Bring Upon Yourself; But Much More Stinging Is The Kind That Is Brought Upon You.**

2. **Merely Having A Need Doesn't Move The Hand Of God!**

3. **The Crowd Always Has An Opinion About Your Passion; They Don't Know Your Pain.**

4. **One Of The Greatest Freedoms You Must Seek Is The Freedom From Human Opinion.**

5. **Jesus Always Wants To Be Chosen.**

6. **Be Wary Of Those Dithering "Seeing People". Every Season Has Them!**

7. **Find Your Shout Of Faith!**

Chapter 10
A PECULIAR FAITH

"And at midnight Paul and Silas prayed, and sang praises unto God..."

Acts 16:25

The Apostle Paul was on his second missionary journey, strengthening churches all the way from Asia to Europe. God was guiding him, closing and opening doors as he pioneered in this never before reached territory. It was during this time that he met his spiritual son, Timothy, who would pastor Asia's largest church, and the physician Luke whom many believe to have penned the largest of the gospels and the book of Acts. Paul would also meet Lydia, a businesswoman who was instrumental in the founding of a powerful church in Thyatira.

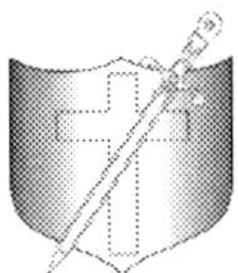

Paul and his companion Silas were entrenched in one particular community. For days, a demonized girl followed them. The evil spirit declared through her, *"These are the servants of the Most High God, who proclaim to us the way of salvation."* (Acts 16:17, NKJV)

What the evil spirit was saying was actually a truth: they were servants of the Most High God, and yes they had come to proclaim the way of salvation. But after a few days, Paul was irritated and said, *"I command you in the name of Jesus Christ to come out of her." And he came out that very hour.* "(Acts 16:18b, NKJV)

Trouble ensues: the girl's parents were using her gift to tell fortunes and earn a living by it. When the evil spirit leaves, so does their source of income. The parents have Paul and Silas arrested and they are falsely charged as follows: *"These men, being Jews, exceedingly trouble our city; and they teach customs which are not lawful for us, being Romans..."* (Acts 16:20-21, NKJV)

Well, the crowds turn on them; the magistrates hear the biased, bogus charges, and find the men of God guilty.

Paul and Silas are disrobed and beaten with rods. Verse 23 says, *"And they laid many stripes upon them."*

Although the Jews had a limit of thirty-nine stripes for their prisoners, the Romans had no such restriction and, therefore, Paul and Silas must have received a savage beating. In fact, Paul may be referring to this instance when he later writes about his persecutions in 2 Corinthians 11:23, by saying he received, *"Stripes beyond* measure."

Was it forty or fifty stripes or more? The fact is these guys were severely scourged and inhumanely punished. The Bible says, *"When they had struck them with many blows, they threw them into prison, commanding the jailer to guard them securely; and he, having received such a command, threw them into the inner prison and fastened their feet in the stocks."*

Serving Jesus Does Not Insulate Us From Hardships.

Stocks were wooden beams with multiple holes for legs. The captors would force the feet of the prisoner into the holes, apart in such a way so as to cause the utmost discomfort and pain. In fact, sometimes, if they were tight enough, prisoners could lose a foot or leg from the loss of blood circulation. Here is what I personally find interesting: there are only two groups of people in recorded history that commonly used stocks for punishment—the Romans and the Baganda people in Uganda—my tribe. Crazy, right?

So, imagine Paul and Silas, beaten to near unconsciousness with their backs probably shredded to the bone. As if that wasn't enough, they were locked up in the inner jail (or maximum prison); their feet fastened in painful stocks and, in addition, were assigned a jailer to guard them.

Sometimes It Looks And Feels Like God Has Abandoned Us.

Doesn't that seem extreme to you? I think it was. What could a couple of unarmed guys do to withstand mighty Rome? Fight their way out, or somehow escape? Did they fear that fellow Jews would come and break them out of the maximum-security inner jail? Likely not! I suspect they were afraid of something supernatural. Could it be they had heard about how an angel broke Peter out of jail? Can you hear them saying, "Hey if you imprison one of these Christians or Jesus-people, you better make sure they are guarded, because weird stuff has happened?"

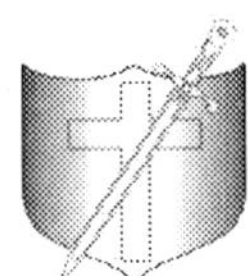

Verse 25 says, *"And at midnight Paul and Silas prayed, and sang praises unto God: and the prisoners heard them."*

If the prison walls could speak, can you imagine what they would say?

> *"What? Prayers? Wait a minute! Those vibrations are unusual. That pitch isn't normal. It isn't a scream, shrill, or a yell. Is that a song? People don't do that here. No one sings in here. This is a place of tears, sorrow, cussing and excruciating* pain. *There is no singing here!"*

What a strange sound it must have been.

And what about the fellow prisoners, those hardened criminals? Can you imagine what they were thinking?

> *"Surely they are not singing. You don't sing here! Who are these guys who sing in the midst of such pain and humiliation? How does a man sing when he should cry? Their joy must come from somewhere else. And here is a more important question, how come they sing to a god who has obviously abandoned them and failed to protect them?"*

Keep in mind that praise is only ascribed for accomplishment or given in honor and celebration of some achievement. Paul and Silas were ascribing praise to a god who obviously hadn't been good to them that day. I am sure they asked God's protection that morning. You bet they prayed that angels would surround them and keep them from danger or the snares of the enemies of the gospel. I am certain they had plans that evening—plans to serve God, no doubt. I am certain they did not expect the day to turn out so unfavorably. God had lifted His hand of protection from them, and they had been arrested, brutalized, and jailed like animals.

Anyone Can Sing At Noon, But Can You Sing At Midnight?

The mistreatment would normally provoke grumbling, complaining, questioning and maybe regret. But, instead, they praise God! No way! Indeed, these guys are different; even peculiar!

Paul wrote to his spiritual prodigy, Titus, "*...and purify unto Himself a peculiar people.*" (Titus 2:14, emphasis)

Peter himself later writes, *"But ye are a chosen generation, a royal priesthood, an holy nation, a peculiar people..."* (1 Peter 2:9)

Yes, we are a peculiar people. That word "peculiar" means *odd, strange, weird, unusual, abnormal, atypical, and even eccentric*! Yes, Glory to God, we are weird. Stop and say it right now:

"I AM WEIRD!"

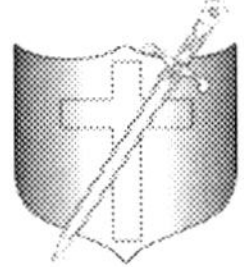

Friends, it is easy to praise God when things are going great; when you've got a great job, feel like you are married to the best spouse in the world, when your kids act like perfect little angels, or when your body is in tip-top shape. Any one of us can sing praise to God when we see His provisions, His protection, and His goodness. But can you praise God when things go south? Can you sing praises through calamity? You can easily sing at noon, while the sun is out … but can you sing at midnight?

Can you sing:

- When there is trouble?
- When you don't have a job?
- When you are sick?
- When your marriage is crumbling?
- After your teenager has run away from home?
- When your home is being taken away from you?
- When you are lonely, abandoned and rejected?
- When you are being discriminated against?
- In the face of betrayal?

Can you sing at midnight?

Christians do! We do, because we are weird. You do, while everyone is looking and wondering why you are at church after losing everything you own. You smile because, even still, you love God! Yeah, but He didn't protect you. Your husband went away to war and was killed, leaving you with two toddlers. So, really, you should be angry at the Lord. But you are not. Instead, you sing.

We used to sing back in Uganda that:

Ye Mulungi (Oh God is good)

Ye Mulungi (Oh God is good)

Ye Mulungi (Oh God is good)

Katonda wange (He's so good to me!)

Back then, we often had no food to eat for three days. Of course, God could provide like He had done so many times previously. I had seen Him miraculously multiply small meals to feed our household of ten. On several occasions, food had been delivered to our door anonymously in the midst of a shower of bullets and indiscriminate bombing outside—angels at work! But, there were also times when we'd go three days without anything to eat. We'd go to church and still sing and dance before the Lord with gratitude. Did we wonder why He hadn't provided for us? Of course. But we still sang the song of the Lord!

God is good, not because I saw His goodness today. He is good because I *know* He is good. He is good not because He performed miracles for me today. I praise God not just for His accomplishments or mighty works, but because of who He is: *Good*!

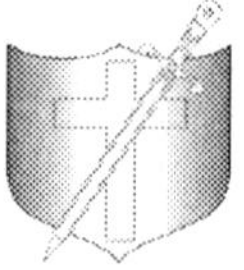

Verse 26 of Acts Chapter 16 says:

> *"Suddenly there was a great earthquake, so that the foundations of the prison were shaken; and immediately all the doors were opened and everyone's chains were loosed."* (NKJV)

The timing, intensity, epicenter and the impact of this earthquake lets us know it was God who shook that jail, right? This is exactly what the

Romans feared. The prison foundations were shaken so hard, all the chains were loosed and doors opened.

> *"And the keeper of the prison, awaking from sleep and seeing the prison doors open, supposing the prisoners had fled, drew his sword and was about to kill himself."*(Verse 27, NKJV)

Why was the keeper sleeping? Well, he must have felt confident his prisoners were not going anywhere. Remember, they had been beaten to a pulp, had their feet fastened with stocks and were confined to the inner jail. Why not take a nap?

We Praise God, Not Only Because Of His Wondrous Works, But Because Of Who He Is!

But when he woke up and saw the unlocked prison doors, he rightly assumed a prison break. Why wouldn't all those hardened, unchained criminals not simply walk out to freedom? The Greeks and the Romans executed jailers after prison breaks, regardless of the circumstances. So, this guy thought killing himself was the honorable thing to do.

> "*But Paul called with a loud voice, saying, 'Do yourself no harm, for we are all here.'"*(Verse 28, NKJV)

While we might understand Paul and Silas staying to maybe preach to the jailer, what about these hardened criminals? Why didn't they leave? Could it be they felt safer with Paul and Silas? Better to stay with these peculiar guys than wander out there in uncertainty.

> *"Then he called for a light, ran in, and fell down trembling before Paul and Silas. And he brought them out and said, "Sirs, what must I do to be saved?"*(Verse 29, 30)

Let me put this question another way:

> *"Guys, I beat you today. I mocked you for your faith. I saw you humiliated, disrobed, chained and stocked. I saw you cry, but I also saw you pray. I saw you sing and I knew you were done for. Now I see how powerful your God is. How can I be like you? How can I be peculiar like you? What can I do to be saved?"*

The jailer asked the question knowing what befalls Christians. He knew what happens to converts of the Way, how they were persecuted, beaten and sometimes executed.

The World May Call Us Weird. The Holy Spirit Calls Us Peculiar.

> *"So they said, 'Believe on the Lord Jesus Christ, and you will be saved, you and your household.' Then they spoke the Word of the Lord to him and to all who were in his house. And he took them that same hour of the night and washed their stripes. And immediately he and all his family were baptized. Now when he had brought them into his house, he set food before them; and he rejoiced, having believed in God with all his household."* (Verse 31-34, NKJV)

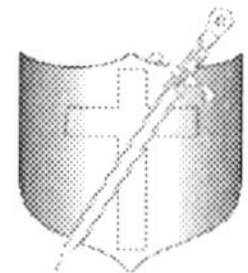

You might be saying, "Dennis I am in jail right now: my health, my life, my family, my kids—it's horrible, It's dark. It's … it's *midnight*! I am struggling to find my song."

This is the Word of the Lord to you:

> *God loves you; He always has. He is more than a provider, sustainer, giver, protector, comforter, or a safety net. Jesus is Lord. If you don't know Him, like the jailer you can right now. Will*

> *you believe on the Lord Jesus Christ? His promise is that you too will be saved!*

Pray this prayer:

> *"Jesus, I believe in You today. I believe You came, died and rose again for me. Come into my life and give it meaning. Make me Your child. Amen."*

For those who know Him, but can't see for the darkness of the night, pray this prayer:

God, I pray You give me courage to sing my song of faith! I declare right now that You are good, even when I don't see it, feel it or experience it. However long this night shall last, I know that not many hours hence, my suddenly *shall happen! May I find fellowship with You today. In spite of my afflictions. I sing:*

> *Ye Mulungi (Oh God is good)*
>
> *Ye Mulungi (Oh God is good)*
>
> *Ye Mulungi (Oh God is good)*
>
> *Katonda wange (He's so good to me!)*

Chapter Truths
A PECULIAR FAITH

1. **Serving Jesus Doesn't Insulate Us From Hardship.**

2. **Sometimes It Looks And Feels Like God Has Abandoned Us.**

3. **Anyone Can Sing At Noon, But Can You Sing At Midnight?**

4. **God Is Good...All The Time!**

5. **We Praise God, Not Only Because Of His Wondrous Works, But Because Of Who He Is!**

6. **The World May Call Us Weird; The Holy Spirit Calls Us Peculiar.**

Chapter 11
A KINGDOM FAITH

"But seek ye first the Kingdom of God, and His righteousness; and all these things shall be added unto you."

Matthew 6:33

"Well, how come God doesn't seem to work as phenomenally here in the West as He does in Africa?"

This is the most common question I am asked when serving in developed nations. As I explained in Chapter Five, I believe it has a lot to do with the desperate conditions we live in. Another reason, in my experience, is the manner of our thinking—we think differently.

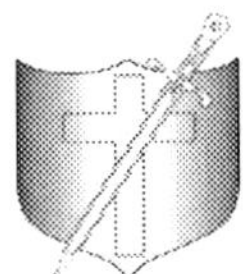

The main form of governance in today's most powerful and dominant western cultures is democracy. A simple definition of democratic governance is one where supreme power is held by the people, under a free electoral system. True democracies are reinforced by two main attributes:

1. Individualism

Even the most unimportant citizen is significant. Everyone gets to have a voice. In fact, the more robust the democracy, the louder the humblest of her voices becomes. Democratic government leaders exist to serve the masses. Every few years, the electorate gets to decide whether or not their leaders have done a good job and, if they haven't, they elect someone else. This is arguably the best form of human governance because quite frankly, humans just haven't quite figured out how to avoid the corruption of power.

2. Choice

Good democracies offer choices and encourage their citizens to determine whom they want to govern them and how they want them to do their jobs.

I remember when I first walked into a full-service restaurant in England. After we got seated, the waitress asked us what we'd like to drink. Well, therein was my first shock. *Why ask? Just tell me whatever you have and I will be fine with it, I thought*. "Pepsi," I muttered with great relief. Where I was raised, almost all soft drinks were called, PEPSI. The giant had a near monopoly in 1970's Kampala.

Citizens In A Democracy Seek To Understand Before They Obey.

As I tried to settle in, I notice the waitress staring at me. Whatever was the problem? Did I mispronounce the word? Then she asked a most disarming question: "What kind of Pepsi do you want?" What? What other kind of Pepsi was there? Ayayaya. She noticed my perplexed blank stare, and decided to help me out.

"Diet or regular?"

Of course, I didn't know what diet was, so I said, "Regular." I think I am still healing from that trauma.

A couple of years later, we flew to America and on the first night in Chicago, we thought it would be a treat to accompany our hosts to a Dominick's grocery store. I will never forget that night.

"What kind of cereal do you guys eat?" Drake asked. *What other kind is there*, I thought.

"Corn Flakes of course!" In Uganda, all cereal was called Corn Flakes.

You should have seen our jaws drop when we walked down the cereal aisle for the very first time. We would have never guessed there were so many different brands. The same experience happened when we hit the toothpaste aisle. We never knew there was another brand of toothpaste besides Colgate—it's all we had in Uganda. What Choices!

And so, that was my introduction to what has been called the global vanguard of democracy: the United States of America. People have opinions here. There are citizen representatives at every level. If you don't like your leader, you don't have to subject yourself to their authority. Even their president can be impeached. Amazing.

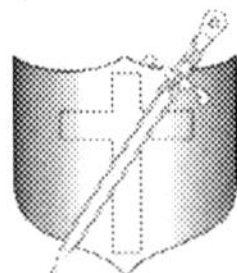

On the other side of the spectrum is the monarchic form of governance where ruler-ship is held by one supreme power; often for life, or until abdication. In addition, the one supreme power is set apart from the subjects. In other words, the king and monarchy is set apart from the common people.

True monarchies are reinforced by two main attributes:

1. Absolute power.

All power is concentrated at the top. The king or queen's word is law. They have no co-governance, no legislative body or regulation system. While democracies provide a voice for their citizenry, monarchies don't. They rule over their subjects, while presidents or prime ministers govern—that's a big difference!

2. Unquestioned obedience.

Citizens of a democracy get to voice their opinions concerning the general direction of their government. If they don't agree, they generally have an option to elect someone else or contribute to some form of organized dissent. In a monarchy, there is no such thing. All decrees are met with unquestioned obedience.

Subjects In A Monarchy Don't Need To Understand Why They Must Obey.

Psalms 147:5, NLT says,

> *"How great is our Lord! His power is absolute! His understanding is beyond comprehension!"*

Absolute power—unchallenged omniscience!

Daniel writes, *"His rule is everlasting, and His kingdom is eternal."* (Daniel 4:34c, NLT)

Sounds like God's ruler-ship is monarchic, doesn't it? Well it is. God is a King, and we are His subjects. Paul declares, *"...Christ... the King of all kings and Lord of all lords."* (1 Timothy 6:15, NLT)

Friends, the Kingdom of God is not a democracy. Therefore, as Christians, we are not citizens of some democracy but subjects of a monarchy. This is vitally important in order to understand faith.

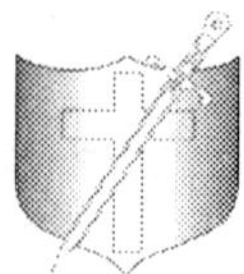

When a king decrees something, the subjects must obey it and then, maybe, seek to understand it. In other words, they don't have to understand it, agree with it or like it. A king's wish is a command. In a democracy, on the other hand, when the president announces a law, the citizens must first understand it, in order to, or before, they obey it. Here are the two paradigms:

Kingdom: HEAR = OBEY = UNDERSTAND (maybe)

Democracy: HEAR = UNDERSTAND = OBEY (maybe)

As an example, say a western government passes a new tax. Its first task is to explain it so citizens will understand it in order to comply. While there are penalties for non-compliance of any law, it is incumbent upon the government to sell the law first. Citizens must understand it before compliance can be expected.

In contrast, if a monarchy decrees a new tax, it has no obligation to explain it. The subjects are simply required to pay the tax and then, perhaps eventually—although not necessarily—they might understand it. These are markedly different systems!

My friends in the West have often asked, *"Dennis, why do you allow those blood-thirsty African dictators to Lord over you? You guys are really smart, strong and capable. Yet you seem to just take this like sitting ducks. What's up with that?"*

Monarchies Cannot Do Democracy Without Fundamentally Changing Their Thinking.

The answer is simple: we filter all governance through monarchic thinking. We are not conditioned to question or challenge leadership. We are too slow or, at best, too reluctant to question their decisions and depose, or vote, them out. Is it any wonder why these dictators flourish? Our leaders are also not used to accountability. Until we change that, we cannot successfully run democratic governments in Africa. In other words, we do democracy horribly wrong because we think: "monarchy". We have unquestioned obedience. Is it any wonder we have dictator after dictator for presidents?

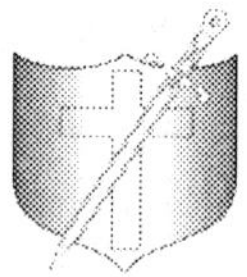

Now, while we cannot practice democracy without fundamentally changing our thinking, we likewise cannot practice kingdom without altering our thinking. Stay with me. You see, while the Africans do democracy really badly, they do Christianity extremely well because it is kingdom. Let me explain…

My friends in the West who live in the world's greatest democracies have a major problem with Christianity because they naturally look at Christianity—as they do everything else—through the filters of democracy.

"I can pick and choose what I want to believe."

"I want to worship when I am in the mood."

"I can't worship with this kind of musical style."

"I don't feel like going to church today."

"My pastor isn't as exciting anymore."

"This church is boring so let's move to that one."

If thoughts like this consume you, you are probably looking at your Christian experience through the filter of a democratic mindset.

Friends, true Christians worship God because they thrive on it. We give to God because we live by it. We obey even if we don't understand it. This makes a big difference.

When you say to an African, "Jesus wants to heal you," they will likely answer, "Amen! So, how can I receive my healing?" We are generally not interested in how the healing will happen or what formula to apply in order to receive it. We hear, we believe, and then seek to understand, if possible—Kingdom thinking!

Democracies Cannot Do Kingdom Without Fundamentally Changing Their Thinking.

I am a witness to some of the most incredible, mind-blowing manifestations of miracles, signs, and wonders.

A lady came for prayer one morning and said to me, "Pastor Dennis, I would like you to pray for us…my husband and I need to have children. We have been trying for twelve years." So, I prayed and I just said, "God, thank you that you open this womb in Jesus' name."

As she turned to leave, the Holy Spirit told me to tell her, "Woman, you shall have a child by this time next year."

She simply replied, "Amen," as they walked away.

I came back the following year and indeed there was a baby. Of course, I was excited and glorified God. She then proceeded to tell me their story.

> *"Pastor Dennis, when you prayed for us, it was impossible to have a baby."* I nodded, thinking, Yeah I think you told me it was. *"Well, you don't understand how amazing this is. A year prior, my uterus had been removed. It was not possible for me to ever bear any children! But I believed the Word of the Lord when you told me He would bless me with a child. A couple weeks after prayer, I felt nauseous, so I asked my husband to take me to the doctor for a checkup. The doctor insisted I was imagining it, and refused to give me a pregnancy test. This was quite understandable, since he was the one who had removed my uterus. But, I would not stop asking so he indulged me and did*

the test. To his shock, and our joy, I was indeed pregnant! After many tests, it was confirmed: God had supernaturally created a new uterus in my body. So... here she is: our miracle baby! Will you please bless our baby?"

That's Kingdom faith, isn't it? Why even ask for prayer to have a child when you don't have a uterus? But that's how a regular person would process it. Not me or you! Kingdom-minded believers know God's ways don't have to make sense. They know His Word is true no matter the circumstances. Jesus still performs miracles today!

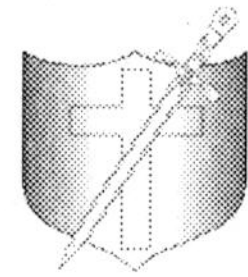

My mother once told me this amazing story:

"Son, I used to go hang out at the palace with my cousins. We had family relations with the king and what an incredible experience it was! Getting to have the king's audience was the most coveted thing in the land. Once someone received that official notification, the first thing they did was to familiarize themselves with the king and his history—his conquests and victories; only the good stuff of course!

"Next, they prepared a gift. You never, ever showed up to see the king without a gift. The farmer was to bring a sample of their most bountiful yield. The fisherman would spend all night trying to catch the biggest fish they could. The cattle-keeper would bring their fattest calf or cow—only the best for the king!

So, you showed up for your appointment and the first order of the day was to receive your gift at the palace entrance. As soon as you stepped into the outer court, you began to literally shout the praises of the king: 'Oh our great king is the mightiest of warriors. He led our armies to war against vicious tribes far and away. Had it not been for his wisdom, we would not have so great a kingdom. We would have been annexed by foreigners and our women would have been taken and sold into slavery!' At that point, everyone knew exactly why you were there: to see the King.

Once you entered the throne room, you must lower your voice, as you were now in the presence of His Majesty, the king of Buganda. He's seated in that very throne room, so you lay prostrate on the ground with your face down. You never look a king in the eye. "Oh great king," you say. "I am now in your hands. I tremble in your presence, at your mighty power. Will you please grant the humble request of your subject?" You present your request and rarely does anyone ever leave the king's presence with an unmet petition!"

As I listened to her story, I was filled with joy. Listen to this scripture:

> *"No one should appear before the Lord empty-handed. Each of you must bring a gift in proportion to the way the Lord your God has blessed you."* (Deuteronomy 16:16, 17, NIV)

That sounds like kingdom protocol. You don't want to come before the Lord without a gift because you are presenting yourself before a King! And I like that second sentence, "... in proportion to the way the Lord God has blessed you." So, none of this nonsense some preachers tout: "God wants to bless whoever will sow $1,000 right now." That is not our God. We give in proportion to the way the Lord our God has blessed us, because to a truly rich man, for example, $1,000 is nothing, yet it is impossible for a single mother in some remote Kenyan village to give $100. Why would God decree a blessing upon an amount only a select few can afford? He is a just God! That growing trend is totally unbiblical, manipulative and plain evil!

We Must Cheerfully Give In Proportion To The Way God Has Blessed You.

Read this: *"Give unto the Lord the glory due unto His name, bring an offering, come into His courts."* (Psalms 96:8)

Psalms 100:4 says, *"Enter into His gates with thanksgiving and a thank offering and His courts with praise!"* (AMP)

Doesn't that sound like an entrance to a palace?

Worship Is A Critical Part Of Kingdom Protocol.

Friends, praising God is a critical part of kingdom protocol. When the worship service begins, it's not some warmer-upper, or time-filler before the main event (the all-important sermon); it is all part of the main event. We enter His gates with thanksgiving; we enter His courts with praise! In Africa, in some services, all we do is worship. We sing and get to bask in His presence. Often times, spectacular miracles happen during worship as we sing and dance in His courts.

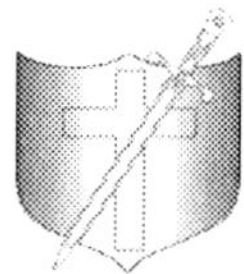

Jesus said, *"But seek ye first the kingdom of God and His righteousness and all these things shall be added unto you."* (Matthew 6:33)

Kingdom subjects know it is their king's pleasure to take care of them. When a king hosts a fellow monarch, everything must look clean and pristine. The way a kingdom looks is a reflection of the glory of the king. In fact, it was scandalous for visiting kings to see roadside beggars or paupers; it made the kingdom look poor and hurt the king's reputation.

It is the good pleasure of our King of kings, Jesus Christ, to care for us, but we get to seek Him and His Kingdom first. The bottom line is this: Kingdom subjects have absolute faith in their king, whether they understand his ways or not. As King's kids, we must learn to say:

> *"I thank You Lord because You are good all the time! I praise You even though I don't understand what's going on right now—because I don't have to. As Your child, I shall simply obey Your decrees because they are good for me! I trust in Your goodness whether I see it right now or not. I am blessed, not because I see Your blessing, but because You* say *I am!"*

We Have Absolute Faith In Our Absolute God, Whether We See His Goodness Today Or Not!

"Dennis, what if I am going through hell right now?" you might ask. Someone reading this might be experiencing adversity, painful pangs of poverty, political anarchy, sex slavery, or some unspeakable storm. Yes, I say, God is still good—all the time!

Here is one of my favorite Bible verses: *"For My thoughts are not your thoughts, neither are your ways My ways, saith the Lord."* (Isaiah 55:8)

The New Living Translation is even more sobering; it says:

> *"My thoughts are nothing like your thoughts, says the Lord, and My ways are far beyond anything you could imagine."*

That's really powerful. God is telling us He doesn't think like us; we think too small. In my experience, even when I was devoid of all hope my situation was far from hopeless. God always has something else up His *big* sleeve! When I prayed for a promotion, I didn't know I had to be fired first. When I asked for faith, I didn't know it would come by way of betrayal and serial calamities. So now I choose to trust Him. This is Kingdom faith!

Chapter Truths
A KINGDOM FAITH

1. **Citizens In A Democracy Seek To Understand Before They Obey.**

2. **Subjects In A Monarchy Don't Need To Understand Why They Must Obey.**

3. **Monarchies Cannot Do Democracy Without Fundamentally Changing Their Thinking.**

4. **Democracies Cannot Do Kingdom Without Fundamentally Changing Their Thinking.**

5. **We Must Cheerfully Give In Proportion To The Way God Has Blessed Us.**

6. **Worship Is A Critical Part Of Kingdom Protocol.**

7. **We Have Absolute Faith In Our Absolute God, Whether We See His Goodness Today Or Not!**

Chapter 12
A BOUNTEOUS FAITH

"And He said, 'He that shewed mercy on him.' Then said Jesus unto him, 'Go, and do thou likewise.'"

Luke 10:37

> *"And, behold, a certain lawyer stood up, and tempted Him, saying, Master, what shall I do to inherit eternal life?"* (Luke 10:25)

Tempted Him! Yes, that's right. That was common in Jesus' meetings. Remember, before Jesus made His disruptive entrance, the religious hierarchy had it made. There were 613 commandments given to the children of Israel that no one could really keep. In fact, several times, Jesus directly called them out about their hypocrisy.

This lawyer was probably a Pharisee, because they were the ones who believed in life after death. Jesus pointed him back to the law, God's established counsel, in Deuteronomy and Leviticus:

"He said unto him, 'What is written in the law?"

> "And He answering said, *Thou shalt love the Lord thy God with all thy heart, and with all thy soul, and with all thy strength, and with all thy mind; and thy neighbor as thyself. And He said unto him, 'Thou hast answered right: this do, and thou shalt live.'"* (Verse 27)

Of course, the lawyer is supposed to know the law, so was he embarrassed? Did he feel snubbed? Was Jesus' response too simplistic for him? He asked another probing question, still to trap Jesus:

"Well, then, who is my neighbor?"

Jesus was prompted to tell him this beautiful parable:

> *"And Jesus answering said, 'A certain man went down from Jerusalem to Jericho, and fell among thieves, which stripped him of his raiment, and wounded him, and departed, leaving him half dead.'"* (Verse 30)

The distance from Jerusalem to Jericho is twenty miles. But there was a place mid-journey inhabited by violent robbers known as *The Way of the Blood.* That is where this man was beaten, stripped, robbed, and left for dead.

> *"And by chance there came down a certain priest that way: and when he saw him, he passed by on the other side. And likewise a Levite, when he was at the place, came and looked on him, and passed by on the other side."* (Verse 31, 32)

Being Religious Doesn't Necessarily Engender Compassion.

Wait a minute—these were the religious elite of the day! Here was a wounded and dying man, but they passed him by. They were the same race, nationality, and religion as this fellow Jew; they should have helped. In fact, they were obligated to help. Leviticus 19 says, *"You shall love a stranger."*

It was their duty to stop. And remember, Priests and Levites worked in the temple. They were to be the epitome of godliness, kindness and benevolence.

But they passed this man by.

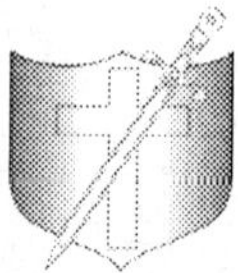

> *"But a certain Samaritan, as he journeyed, came where he was: and when he saw him, he had compassion on him"* (Verse 33)

Samaritans were a different race, a different nationality, and a different religion. Samaritans and Jews did not get along. The Jews believed they were superior to the Samaritans and treated them as substandard Gentiles. This man had every right to just walk away and maybe even say, "Serves you right, you filthy Jew!" But the Bible says he did several things:

> *"And went to him, and bound up his wounds, pouring in oil and wine, and set him on his own beast, and brought him to an inn, and took care of him. And on the morrow when he departed, he took out two pence, and gave them to the host, and said unto him, Take care of him; and whatsoever thou spendest more, when I come again, I will repay thee."*(Verse 34, 35)

Let's examine this closely:

1. He didn't pass him by, but had compassion on him.
2. He reached out to him and touched him: a sign of genuine care.
3. He bound up his wounds, pouring in oil and wine, which was the first-aid of the day.
4. He set him on his own beast, which speaks of proximity and closeness.
5. He brought him to an inn, which means he interrupted his agenda for a considerable amount of time.
6. He spent his resources—two days wages—on his care and recovery, basically saying, "I am all-in!"

Now, in order for the Samaritan to do all this, he had to do three very important things:

First, he had to cross social barriers and overcome prejudices; the feelings of ostracism and political correctness. He had to say to himself, *I will go help this man, even if he belongs to a class of people who hate my guts.*

Real Compassion Is Visible.

Second, he had to be willing to take significant risks. He should not have stopped, as this was a dangerous way; you don't stop by *The Way of the Blood.* If you were fortunate enough to make it through that strip without being robbed or killed, you kept going. But he stopped. What if this was an ambush? What if he was being manipulated?

Third, he had to make significant sacrifices. It must have been inconvenient for him to suspend his own journey. It was no doubt disruptive to help this Jewish man. Can you imagine having to lift a limp, bloodied body of a stranger up on your donkey? The whole ordeal must have been time consuming and costly—a sacrifice!

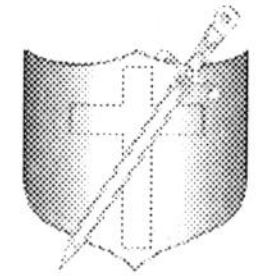

Jesus posed a question: *"Which now of these three, thinkest thou, was neighbor unto him that fell among the thieves?"* (Verse 36)

His question invokes a different perspective. He doesn't just ask who was more loving, but which one was more responsive to the need at hand.

The lawyer responded, "He that showed mercy on him." (Verse 37)

That's it—end of discussion.

Friends, our neighbors are those in need, regardless of their affinities. "But he's black, and I'm white, I don't know." Well, color is just a matter of pigmentation. Inside, all of us have the same elements that make for a living, human being.

I come from a history of vicious tribalism. I remember as a kid I was always told, "Watch out for those Acholis, and Langis. You can't quite ever trust them." My very best friend, Robert Okema, was from one of those tribes, and I remember my Baganda friends looking at me suspiciously, "Why are you risking your life? Why would you even bring him to your house? He is an Acholi!" Relatives would caution, "Don't you dare go to Robert's house. You just don't know; they might eat you." All these crazy things we humans come up with to reinforce prejudices. In fact, I was never supposed to marry someone of a different tribe. Well, I did far worse: I married a woman of a different color. I married a Romanian all the way from Europe. Scared them to bits, but, eventually, our marriage became a powerful testimony and lesson to my circle of friends and to the entire country.

We Are Compelled To Love Those Who Don't Look Like Us, Behave Like Us, Or Live Like Us!

Our neighbors are those in need regardless of their nationality, religion, or status. You ought to love them even if they look different. They are your neighbors even if they believe differently. We are called to an altruistic faith.

Matthew 5:20 says, *"For I say unto you, that unless your righteousness exceeds the righteousness of the Scribes and the Pharisees, you will by no means enter the kingdom of heaven."* (NKJV)

That's a very powerful statement. Jesus talked about two men considered righteous vanguards of the law, the Priest and the Levite. They walked by a man in desperate need. His admonition in Matthew was this: "Unless your righteousness is greater than some cosmetic exercise, you will not enter the Kingdom of heaven. You can't be part of me" (paraphrased). Sobering, isn't it?

Is your righteousness a "Priestly" righteousness, which only loves those who believe like you? Is it a "Levitical" righteousness, which only loves those who act like you? Or is it a "Samaritanic" righteousness, which loves whoever is in need?

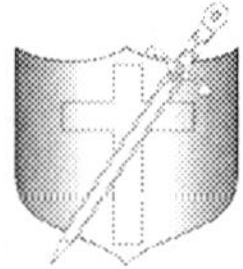

Jesus ends the conversation with a stern instruction: "Go and do likewise." That's it—the prescription to inheriting the Kingdom of God.

In other words, "You go and love like a Samaritan. You are to love those who are not like you, who don't share your beliefs."

Does Your Righteousness Transcend Your Religion?

I remember going up into the mountains of Siberia on a mission trip, to a particular village where they had never seen a black person. The kids would come up to me and try to rub off my dark color; it was pretty cool. I was definitely different all right, but these guys loved me. I sat down to eat with them, drinking what people in the West would call spoiled or stale milk, and broke bread with them late into the night.

You are called to:

1. Love those who are not like you. Yes, the bad, the rebellious, the criminals, the nerds, the geeks, the fat, the awkward, and the recalcitrant.

2. Love those who don't look like you. Yes, the black, the white, Hispanics, the scruffy, the clean, the smelly, the ruffians, and the degenerates.

3. Love those who don't believe like you. Yes, the homosexuals, the liberals, the conservatives, the atheists, the radicals, the democrats, the republicans, the socialists, the communists and even the Islamists.

Because faith—true bounteous faith—compels us to love those who are not like us, who don't look like us, and who don't believe like us!

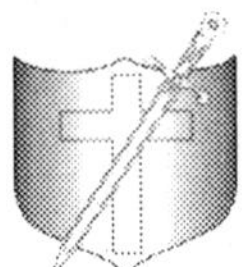

Perhaps you are saying, "God, I have been hurt by these people," or, "My experience with people who believe like that hasn't been good at all!" Or, you might even have horror stories: "Hey, I was molested by my white neighbor, so white people and I just don't get along!" One of our closest friends was gang-raped by a black gang, so, in the natural, she really should not be anywhere close to me. We should not be friends since I should naturally trigger those fears within her. But look what the Lord has done!

We Are Called To An Altruistic Faith Which Is Selfless And Self-Sacrificing.

1 John 3:16 says, *"Hereby perceive we the love of God, because He laid down His life for us: and we ought to lay down our lives for the brethren."*

This verse describes *Agape* love. It is the highest type of love, the only kind of love that can cause a human being to lay down their life for another. This love does not respond naturally. It does not offend or hurt. It isn't selfish or in it for what it can get out of it. It has absolutely no strings attached to it. It other words, it's pure, selfless love—the God-kind of love.

John goes on to say: *"My little children, let us not love in word, neither in tongue; but in deed and in truth."* (Verse 18)

Agape love is a *doing* love. Just like God loved us and "agape'd" us, likewise, we agape those in our world.

"So, how do I get this love?" you might ask. Paul writes, *"Follow after charity."* (1 Corinthians 14:1)

The word "follow" here is the Greek word *dioko*. It means *to pursue*. This means one must run after Agape love. Unfortunately, it just doesn't come naturally to us fallen humans; we are naturally selfish. We tend to look for self-benefit. We give because we hope to get something in return.

But here is the good news: as born again children of God, we have God's love inside of us. John actually says we have God's seed inside of us (1 John 3:9). That is powerful! Think about it for a second: Agape lives in us! Glory to God! The question, then, is: will you let the seed of God produce within you God's perfect love? Will you allow Jesus to break down those barriers and truly become Lord of your life? Once you really do that—and I mean *really* do that—the Holy Spirit will introduce you to a new faith, that bounteous faith that releases His Agape love, the kind of love that knows no barriers; that altruistic, selfless love of God!

Chapter Notes
A BOUNTEOUS FAITH

1. **Being Religious Doesn't Necessarily Engender Compassion.**

2. **Real Compassion Is Visible.**

3. **We Are Compelled To Love Those Who Don't Look Like Us, Behave Like Us, Or Live Like Us!**

4. **Does Your Righteousness Transcend Religion?**

5. **We Are Called To An Altruistic Faith Which Is Selfless And Self-Sacrificing.**

Chapter 13
A STEADFAST FAITH

"Blessed is anyone who does not stumble on account of Me."

Matthew 11:6 (NIV)

"For he shall be great in the sight of the Lord, he shall drink no wine, no strong drink, he shall be filled with the Holy Spirit even from his mother's womb and many of the children of Israel shall he turn unto the Lord their God and he shall go before His face in the Spirit and power of Elijah. He'll turn the hearts of the sons to their father's, the disobedient to walk in the wisdom of the just. To make ready for the Lord a people prepared for Him." (Luke 1:15-17, ASV)

This text refers to the great John the Baptist, a man who was filled with the Holy Spirit even before his birth. His was a prophetic birth; a boy-child fully consecrated to the Lord.

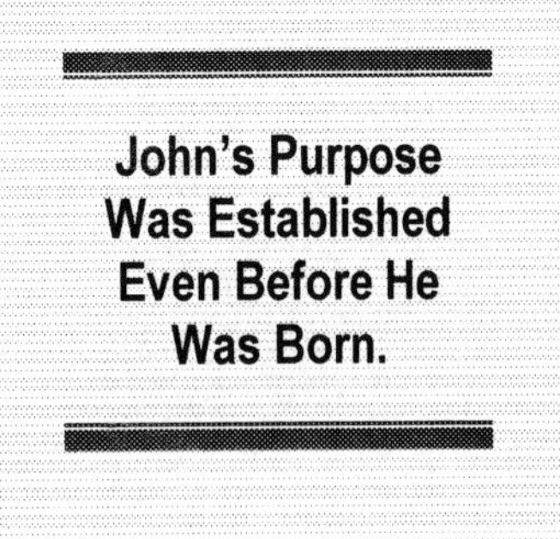

John's Purpose
Was Established
Even Before He
Was Born.

John grew up to be someone who was kind of...*out there*! He wore strange clothing made of camel hair and had a strange diet consisting of honey and locusts. But boy was he a phenomenon! His fame reached throughout Judea and throngs of people would trek to the wilderness to hear his powerful message: REPENT AND BE BAPTIZED!

Baptism? Where did that even come from? Indeed, John was a man of God!

"...And men reasoned in their hearts concerning John, whether

> *haply he were the Christ." (*Luke 3:15, ASV)

The Jews had been anxiously waiting for their soon-coming Messiah, the Christ! With such a powerful, convicting message of repentance, no wonder they thought this might be the Son of David!

John would eventually respond to his inquirers: *"I indeed baptize you with water; but there cometh He that is mightier than I, the latchet of whose shoes I am not worthy to unloose: He shall baptize you in the Holy Spirit and in fire." (*Luke 3:16, ASV)

In other words, "No, guys. I am not He. I am simply His harbinger. I am the preparer of his earthly ministry."

One day, he saw Jesus coming toward him, and decided he would let everyone know what he was talking about. He announced:

> *"Behold the Lamb of God who takes away the sin of the world."* (John 1:29)

In other words, "There! See, there He is! That's the one I have come to prepare for."

Jesus would come to be baptized by John. After some resistance, John accepted and just as He was being baptized, a dove sat upon Him and God spoke audibly: *"...Thou art My beloved Son; in Thee I am well pleased."* (Luke 3:22)

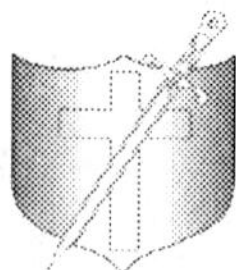

So, Jesus vanished, went away to the wilderness and came back completely different. He was no longer Mary and Joseph's goodly thirty-year-old boy! Jesus was working miracles, healing the sick, casting out demons, cleansing lepers, multiplying food ...oh, and He raised the dead, too!

Consequently, everyone wanted to go see Him. There was not a more compassionate, powerful—and controversial—man to ever walk the face of the earth. As a result, John's crowds began to dwindle. And why wouldn't they? He outright told them Jesus was greater than he and, evidenced by the miracles, there was no better meeting to attend than a Jesus-meeting.

> *"So John's disciples came to him and said, 'Rabbi, the man you met on the other side of the Jordan River, the One you identified as the Messiah, is also baptizing people. And everybody is going to Him instead of coming to us.'"* (John 3:26, NLT)

In other words, "Master, I guess you were right about that man. He is the Messiah all right, but we have a problem. He is now more popular than you, which is hurting us. No one seems to want to come out here to hear you. Jesus has taken your crowd."

John responded and said, most nobly, *"I told you, 'I am not the Messiah. I am only here to prepare the way for Him.' Therefore, I am filled with joy at His success. He must increase, but I must decrease."* (John 3:30, ESV)

I just love this statement, because it has helped center me many times. As the Lord has grown our ministry and put me in front of larger and larger platforms, with every ascent I have had to affirm whom this is about. "Dennis, this is not about you. Jesus *must* increase and you, with your gifts, talents, skill, even experience, *must* decrease."

The Bigger Jesus Gets In Us, The Smaller We Must Become.

John is simply saying, "Guys, I told you I am not He. He is the Messiah…I must get smaller as He gets bigger. My job is done. I came to introduce Him to the world, so His popularity should only make us proud, not envious. Jesus' ascent means our descent!"

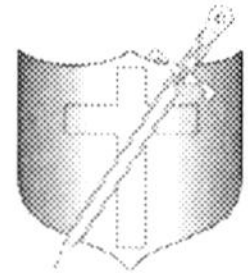

John spoke out against Herod and was jailed for it. Suddenly, things didn't look great for him! As he sat there with his life hanging in the balance, I am sure he probably wondered:

> *"What happened? I had this grand start to my life as a prophet of God. I have lived a devout, righteous life faithfully serving my purpose. Is this it—six months? All my life has been about these short six months? Why am I here? How come things have turned out so badly for me? Shouldn't I be with Jesus right now? My disciples are all scattered. Does Jesus care that I am here? Isn't He supposed to set me free from this yoke?"*
>
> *"...Now when John had heard in the prison the works of Christ..." (*Matthew 11:2)

While he sat there on death row, John heard of the wonders of Jesus, the miracles and tremendous healings. He pondered his station, "Surely all these miracles are leading to something, right? I wonder what's taking Him so long? What if I missed it? What if He is not the One?" As the days rolled on, John couldn't keep the thoughts to himself any longer. *"... he sent two of his disciples, to ask Him, 'Are You the One who is to come, or should we expect someone else?'"* (Matthew 11:2b, 3, NIV)

John Is Certain About His Purpose As Long As He Understands His Circumstances.

Whoa! Wait a minute. Did John just ask that? The man who was called of God and filled with His Spirit, even before his birth? Clearly, in his head, John had a different scenario in mind. He probably expected Jesus to convert the whole region or maybe even topple Rome. Moreover, the Messiah was to come and save His people. But Jesus was not playing to John's script. John's definition of success was markedly different from His. By his question, John was saying, "Now, because my personal life is falling apart, this Jesus must not be the One." Because he couldn't understand Jesus' agenda or direction, he must have thought he had missed it. Suddenly, the great John the Baptist had a major crisis of faith!

If you have been there, like I have many times, you know exactly what John was feeling.

- James has trusted God with his finances for decades. He is a giver and tither, faithfully living within his means. A few months ago, he launched a business and now it has collapsed. "What happened Lord?" he cries. A crisis of faith!

- Gina and Mike decide to tie the knot after months of a rapturous courtship. He is perfect. Her family loves him, and even the pastor approves. They seem made for each other. Two years later, Mike walks out on her. A crisis of faith!

- Bill and Melissa decide to devote the first years of their marriage to hard work. By God's grace, they saved a big enough down payment to buy their dream house. Soon after they moved in, God gave them a baby. Everything is going really well until she loses her job due to a hostile takeover. Suddenly, the housing crisis hits, the bank threatens to take their house away as they sink deeper into debt. A crisis of faith!

- The Smiths thought they raised their kids right. They took them to Sunday school, and did their best to instill a solid work-ethic into them. They were all A-students, high achievers in sports and all-around upstanding kids. But something seems to have completely disrupted their moral compass. One is on drugs, the other—twenty years old—is pregnant with her third child. "What happened, Lord?" they weep. A crisis of faith!

- Michael takes care of his body; he eats well, sleeps eight hours every day, works out and, by any standard, is in super shape. But his annual checkup returns a devastating doctor's report. "God what happened? You promise health to Your children, don't You?" A crisis of faith!

When we hit these crisis points, we feel as though God must not be with us. He is supposed to protect us, save us, cover us, and prosper us, right?

I remember when I hit my first crisis. We had just ended an amazing ten-day crusade in a remote part of Uganda; God had performed so many miracles among us. A local school for the deaf and dumb had bussed in their entire enrollment. That final night, all two hundred kids were miraculously healed; in fact, the school was closed shortly after. So, yeah, did Jesus heal? You bet He did!

When I got home, I walked into the house and noticed my father, who had been battling illness for months, had deteriorated in health. Through his affliction, God had saved him and filled him with the Holy Spirit. He had pledged to serve God as soon as he got better and we were confident his healing was on its way to full manifestation! So, with all the confidence in the world I went straight to his bed and laid hands upon him, commanding, as I had done many times over hundreds of chronically sick people, "Be healed in Jesus' name!"

When Our Circumstances Contradict Our Expectations, They Precipitate Crises Of Faith.

As soon as I walked into the next room to put my bags down, I heard my mother scream: Daddy had just passed away. "No way! He can't; not now," I protested. "He must lead many to Christ. We need our father alive and well! This cannot be of God!"

My father had spent the better part of my childhood battling alcoholism and womanizing. He was a kind man, but was gripped by the enemy. His salvation had already sent tremors around town. He was super excited to be as vocal for Christ as he had been a prodigal from Him. Yet, now he was dead. Why hadn't Jesus healed him? A crisis of faith!

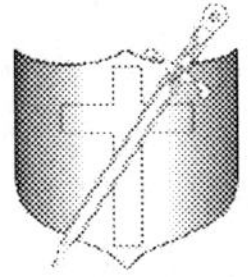

Jesus did not answer John's disciple's question concerning Him being the Messiah. Instead, he said, *"...Go back and report to John what you hear and see: The blind receive sight, the lame walk, those who have leprosy are cleansed, the deaf hear, the dead are raised, and the good news is proclaimed to the poor."*(Matthew 11: 4-5, NIV)

He didn't offer verbal proof of his authenticity. Here is how I read this:

> *"Tell John what you're seeing Me do. Tell John that he must have faith in God even though he doesn't see His hand right now. He has to trust in God even though he is not experiencing His blessings. Instead of nursing his broken soul, My beloved cousin John must focus on My work. He must look at what I am doing, not what I am not doing."*

Instead Of Counting Our Losses, We Must Focus On His Gains.

You can only imagine John's disappointment.

Let's look back at our examples above:

- Instead of focusing on his collapsed business, James must be grateful for his health. Thank God he still had the presence of mind to pick himself up and work his way back.

- Instead of focusing on Mike's infidelity, Gina should be thankful for her best friend Robin. What monetary value can anyone place on a true friend?

- Bob and Melissa must focus on their new bundle of blessing instead of being depressed about their lost home.

- The Smiths must stop blaming themselves and God for their kids' spiritual degradation. They must instead thank God for the grace afforded them, even in their hopeless state of perdition.

- It is pointless for Michael to keep wondering why God didn't protect him from illness. He must instead rejoice that, unlike the billions out there, He has eternal peace with Christ.

Once again, instead of focusing on why we haven't seen God do what we think he ought to do, or even promised to do, we must rejoice in what He *is* doing.

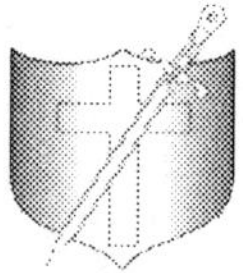

Jesus makes a powerful statement:

> *"Blessed is he who does not stumble on account of Me."* (Verse 6)

Amazing! Blessed are we when Jesus doesn't offend us. Did God not come through for you when you really thought He should? Did you lose your business after you fasted and prayed that God would help you save it? Did your child die even though you felt God would heal them? Did you lose your marriage that God so miraculously gave you? Did your house get repossessed after God had miraculously given it to you? Do you feel like God didn't protect you from your stepbrother's sexual abuse?

Those are some of the devastatingly confusing situations I have heard from broken believers over the last three and a half decades of ministry. The bottom line is: regardless of your estate, you must focus on what God is doing.

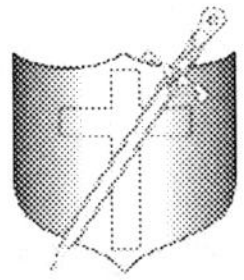

As John's disciples were leaving to take back His response to their master, Jesus turned to the crowd to caution them, lest they think John to be weak or of diminished significance on account of his wavering faith:

> *"What did you go out into the wilderness to see? A reed swayed by the wind? A man dressed in fine clothes? A prophet? Yes, I tell you, and more than a prophet."*(Matthew 11:7-9, NIV)

In other words, Jesus was reminding them of the greatness of John the Baptist! Indeed, he was not a weak man swayed by the wind, even in this moment of doubt and uncertainty. Although he was meagerly dressed, John was a prophet. And, Jesus makes this most startling statement: *"I tell you the truth, of all who have ever lived, none is greater than John the Baptist."* (Verse 11, NLT)

Let's stop there for a minute and think about this. Is Jesus really saying that out of all the prophets, all the patriarchs, the judges, and all the mighty men and women of God who had ever walked the earth, no one was greater than John? That is incredible!

As We Wrestle With *"Why,"* We Must Guard Against Offense At The Lord.

As the disciples were trying to take in the magnitude of that statement, Jesus drew an even bigger conclusion: *"... yet whoever is least in the Kngdom of heaven is greater than he."*

According to our Lord Jesus Christ, the weakest Christian is greater than John the Baptist and therefore all the prophets before him. I always wondered how that could possibly be. Simple…the Bible says: *"But in fact the ministry Jesus has received is as superior to theirs as the covenant of which He is Mediator is superior to the old one, since the new covenant is established on better promises."* (Hebrews 8:6, NIV)

You and I have a better covenant, not like the one written in stone, but one now written on our hearts. We get baptized with the Holy Spirit and with the Fire of God, something no Old Testament prophet, and not even John himself, ever got to experience.

We Are Greater Than John Because We Have A Better Covenant!

Can you even comprehend that? I can't, except by the grace of God, because I know my failings. I know my weaknesses, doubts, unbelief, fears, and shortcomings. Jesus has paid the price for all my sins. While old time prophets had to do certain things to earn the favor of God, we don't. We get to rest in the finished Work of Christ. What a privilege!

Now to those who have stumbled on account of Jesus, I ask that you repent and once again fall into His loving, merciful arms, with all your contradictions, confusion and pain.

Finally, how do you love a God who can, yet won't? How do embrace a God who is completely able to deliver you, yet you still suffer torment? It takes steadfast faith! The faith to quietly submit to His infinite plan for your life, whether it makes sense or not. Do I get impatient trying to figure life out and where things are going? Yup! Do I feel the tremors of unbelief when God doesn't come through like I want Him to? Absolutely. I don't know about you, but I would never want to serve a God I can totally figure out. Thus I long for God to help me walk in steadfast faith!

Chapter Truths
A STEADFAST FAITH

1. **John's Purpose Was Established Even Before He Was Born.**

2. **The Bigger Jesus Gets In Us, The Smaller We Must Become.**

3. **John Is Certain About His Purpose As Long As He Understands His Circumstances.**

4. **When Our Circumstances Contradict Our Expectations, They Precipitate Crises Of Faith.**

5. **Instead Of Counting Our Losses, We Must Focus On His Gains.**

6. **As We Wrestle With "*Why*", We Must Guard Against Offense At The Lord.**

7. **We Are Greater Than John Because We Have A Better Covenant!**

Chapter 14
A TRUSTING FAITH

***"Do not let your hearts be troubled.
Trust in God; trust also in Me."***

John 14:1 (NLT)

I believe in miracles.

I've seen tumors disappear, cancers vanish, limbs grow, eyes open, body parts created, AIDS healed, and the dead raised after prayer. I have seen God miraculously stop rainstorms, cause rain to fall in droughts, fill cars with fuel, supernaturally shield me from bullets and so many unspeakable things—incredible miracles that would blow your mind.

I've also gone without food for days, seen loved ones shot before my eyes, and many a powerful child of God wither away and die from chronic illnesses. This chapter is for those of you who struggle with thoughts like these:

- "Well, I asked for God's blessing, but my business collapsed."
- "I prayed for increase financially but instead, I got fired."
- "I asked for a Godly home, but my marriage is falling apart."
- "I prayed that God would heal me, yet I'm on my death bed."

I call these contradictions. Those experiences which seem to laugh in the face of God's goodness. You know God absolutely heals, provides, delivers, protects, and vindicates, but how come He hasn't? What do you do when your life doesn't mirror what you think a child of God should experience?

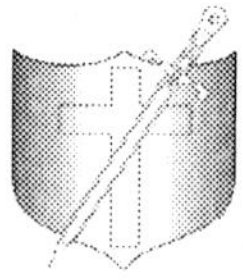

Well, I've heard my fair share of reasons why God didn't come through for me. Many times, I have gone to my pastors, mentors and leaders with my list of contradictions only to come away confused, condemned and worse off. Here is some of what I have been told:

- "You simply don't have enough faith!"
- "You didn't pray correctly."
- "You have un-confessed sin in your life."
- "You just aren't confessing the Word enough."
- "You are using the wrong scriptures."
- "You forgot to plead the blood of Jesus over your life."
- "You didn't put on the armor of God."
- "You are not in alignment with your pastor."
- "You didn't sow enough seed for your need."
- "The enemy has a foothold in your life."

Granted, some of these things could hinder our prayers, but the culprit is often our theology. The fact is, God is amazing, even when we're having problems. Many struggle with this statement because we have been taught that God's goodness is only seen when things are going great or when we are happy.

I hear gross heresy preached around the world, sometimes even on huge platforms, including Christian television: "God wants you well; God wants to give you all the desires of your heart. He just wants to bless you." They make God into some sort of genie, whose main purpose in our lives is to give to us, bless us, and make us well and happy. It is like God's blessings can be unlocked by some combination key. "Here, Mr. Christian, whenever you need anything, just punch this in and if you get it right, you'll never experience problems. You will be blessed, be totally healthy, have amazing relationships and, above all, be super wealthy." How ridiculous!

Sometimes Your Experience Will Contradict Your Faith. Then What?

Here is why I believe this theology is utterly flawed:

1. Your desires come from your heart.

That doesn't sound very profound, but please think about it. Suppose I want something from God, perhaps a promotion. That's a desire and it's from my heart, so does it mean God has to give it to me? Of course not! There's a bigger problem though; listen to what God Himself says about your heart: *"The heart is deceitful above all things and beyond cure. Who can understand it?"* (Jeremiah 17:9, NIV) Mind you, this is God Himself speaking. I'm sure He had Adam and Eve, and the entire history of mankind on His mind when He said that. Who can possibly understand that heart? Can you trust your heart? Why do our hearts want the wrong thing, the wrong woman, the wrong pastime, or the wrong company? Sometimes we want the right thing for the wrong reasons. So, since our hearts sometimes— in fact, often-times—desire the wrong things, how do we expect God to grant us all the desires of our hearts? He can't, if He truly loves us.

God's Primary Focus Is Not To Give To You, Heal You, Or To Bless You. God Is Not Your Genie!

2. Your desires are dictated by your senses.

James is the top salesman at a growing grocery chain store. He knows the manager is quitting, so naturally he wants his position. "I want it," he says, "I am a hard worker and so I really believe God that I will get it. His Word says we shall be heads and not tails, right?" Why? Because in his estimation, the promotion has got to be God's will for his life. But is it?

Your Desires
Originate From
Your Soul.

Maria likes her new associate, Rod. He is a strong man of God, passionate for ministry, and, just like her, burns with a heart for missions. They have so much in common, including the desire to serve among the unreached people in Asia. She has been praying for a husband for ten years now, and Rod seems perfect. He must be God's answer to prayer. But is he?

We desire things based on what we hear, think, and perceive with our finite senses. But Isaiah 55:8 says, *"'My thoughts are nothing like your thoughts,' says the Lord. 'And My ways are far beyond anything you could imagine.'"* (NLT)

Have you ever been glad God didn't answer your prayer? Oh, I have! I thank God for the many unanswered prayers along my journey: those relationships I prayed earnestly for God to preserve, those jobs I had asked God to save, those places I fasted and prayed that God should send me to, those doors my wife and I asked that God would open for us. Thank God he said, "NO, SON!" because today I realize how carnal, misguided and misinformed those desires were.

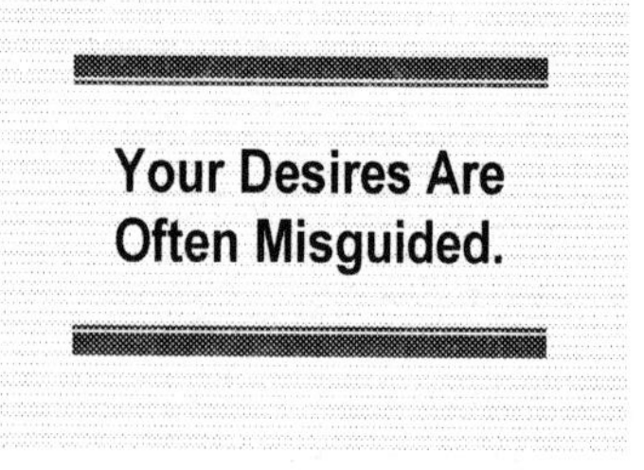
Your Desires Are
Often Misguided.

One of my favorite verses is Jeremiah 29:11, *"For I know the thoughts that I think toward you, says the Lord, thoughts of peace and not of evil, to give you a future and a hope."* (NKJV)

That word "thoughts" is the Hebrew word *makashebeth*, which means *a vivid design*. The word "think" means *to plan* or to *weave.* In other words, God was saying to His servant Jeremiah that He had a vivid design He had weaved for him.

In case you haven't noticed, my friends, God rarely shares His thoughts with us. Even then, our portion is to trust Him, even when it looks like we aren't getting our desires met.

3. Who is Lord?

If God granted every one of your desires—that house you want, that car you claim, those triplets you believe for, and so on—who would be in control of your life? Think about it: you want a red car so you ask God for a red car, and voila, you have a red car! You want that blonde girl for a wife, so you ask for the blonde girl, and swoosh; there is a blonde girl madly in love with you! Who would be in control of your life? God or you? God would be your genie, that lever you pulled and—poof! Who wants such a God? I don't. Here is an even more poignant thought: this god—a god who is at our beck and call—doesn't seem to be the God of the Bible at all. Is that really the God of the universe?

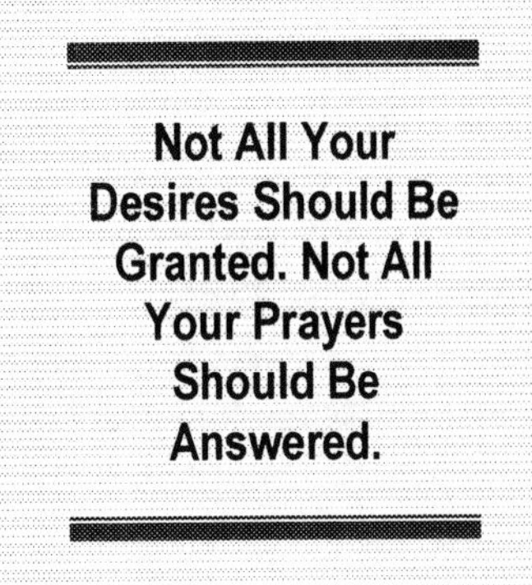

Not All Your Desires Should Be Granted. Not All Your Prayers Should Be Answered.

4. The priceless value of "NO".

If God gave John all his desires, and I mean everything he wanted, he'd be pain-free, stress-free, problem-free, hassle-free, right? But guess what, he would also be a weak, over-gratified spoiled brat. Do you know why? Because all the traits of godliness—patience, kindness, goodness, even faith itself—only come by way of adversity, setbacks and pressure. Let me explain further.

Say John needs patience; ideally, he would pray this way: "Lord, I need patience, so please give it to me now." Do you really think God would simply download patience into John's soul? Not a chance! Patience is born when we are placed in circumstances where we want something so bad or so urgently but cannot have it for a certain amount of time. It is created out of the tension of space between want and fulfillment. So, to get patience John would have to pray this way: "God, please give me three years of hardship."

- Complement a tested man or woman on their admirable patience and they will tell you how God placed them in circumstances of tension and painful lingering.

- Show me a faithful brother, and I will show you a man who bears the scars of betrayal and painful duplicity.

- A trusting woman knows the anguish of uncertainty. That is how faith is born. It is incubated in the midst of ambiguity!

Paul writes, *"Not only so but we also glory in our sufferings because we know that suffering produces perseverance, perseverance produces character and character hope."* (Romans 5: 3-4, NIV)

What is Paul saying? It is through the gateway of suffering that we gain hope. Oh, how many times have I prayed such dangerous prayers like, "God teach me how to love You more." He didn't say, *"Alright son, close your eyes: whoosh! There's love, there's love from Me."* Instead, a season was scheduled during which I was pressured and desperate, with only one solace: my Lord. As the season stretched on, I learned the value of the quiet wait, and its nectar produced within me a love for my One and only Heavenly Father!

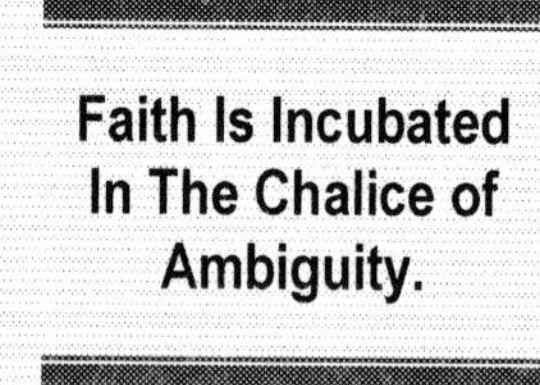

Faith Is Incubated
In The Chalice of
Ambiguity.

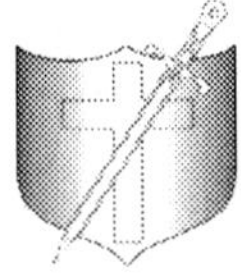

Friend, your faith has been shipwrecked because you expected God to do what you wanted, when you wanted and how you wanted. Many of you are frustrated because God didn't jump when you wanted Him to jump. Of course, it now feels like He wasn't faithful, or maybe that He let you down.

My sons love video games. What if they said, "Daddy, you don't love us because we asked you for a video game last week and you didn't give it to us?" I'd be distraught. They should know that I love them whether I give them what they want or not. Sounds simplistic, but compare then to this scenario:

Strange That We Get Shocked When God Lovingly Withholds For Our Good; When He Acts Like God.

Mary prays, "Father, all my girlfriends are getting married. I have been asking you for a husband for seven years now. Why, Lord? Why am I still single? You must not love me." The fact is God knows when Mary is really ready to be thrust into the most selfless relationship on earth: marriage. And, what *if* He doesn't want Mary to get married at all? Then what? Is He a mean God?

"Lord, I want to get pregnant." Are you ready for sleepless nights and additional pressure on your young marriage? Only the Giver knows.

"Lord, I am ready for that promotion. Give it to me!" What *if* that promotion isn't good for you? What *if* the company is about to go bankrupt and the best course of action is to get out now and get another job? Only the Giver knows.

"Lord, help me land that big distribution deal." What *if* you can't handle that kind of wealth? What *if* you will fall away due to the distractions of opulence? Do you think the Giver will grant your request just to please you?

What I'm saying is, oftentimes, our prayers are not answered—not because God is mean. He isn't uncaring because He didn't do what we wanted, when we wanted or how we wanted. Sometimes, God is just God. He'll do what He wants, how He wants and, of course, *if* He wants. Now, I know this is hard for some of us to read. Some of you probably wish you could email me and school me on our rights as believers, and how Christ has already freely given us all things. Please don't! It is time we learned to separate God from His stuff. God is good even if we didn't see it today. He is good even if we aren't experiencing it right now. Let's not get shocked when God acts like God. We've invited Him to be Lord of our lives, right? Well, then we can't have it both ways, can we? The bottom line is: Jesus is either Lord of our lives, or we are.

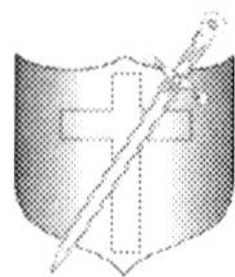

In the book of John, we read how the disciples were about to part from their beloved Friend. They had left family, friends, possessions and honor to follow Him. He was supposed to be there for them, maybe even topple Rome and make them governors, but now He was telling them how He was going to leave and how they would have to meet with persecutions and trials. They were greatly distressed, anxious and perplexed; their countenances probably showed it.

Jesus proceeded to minister consolations to them, as their terrible circumstances warranted. Bible commentator Albert Barnes writes:

> *"There is nowhere to be found a discourse so beautiful, so tender, so full of weighty thoughts so adapted to produce comfort as that which occurs herewith."*[7]

Jesus says, "*Do not let your hearts be troubled. Trust in God, trust also in Me.*" (John 14:1, NLT)

Interestingly, Jesus didn't remove the uncertainties. He didn't tell them, "Guys, you know what, it's not going to be so bad." Instead, He prescribes a pivotal choice: to trust or to panic.

Jesus Promises Comfort—Not From Trouble, But In Spite Of It.

Trust: the birthplace of a vibrant relationship with our God. Since He is completely outside of our sphere of understanding, the only way to relate to Him is through trust. But trust cannot exist without uncertainty. Until you're uncertain, you cannot trust. We trust Him because we don't know what He is really going to do; but we do know it is for our good!

Then Jesus said, *"In My Father's house are many mansions; if it were not so, I would have told you. I go to prepare a place for you. And if I go and prepare a place for you, I will come again and receive you to Myself; that where I am, there you may be also. And where I go you know, and the way you know."* (Verse 2, 3, NKJV)

He paints a fantastical picture of this idyllic and sublime place. He was saying, "Just hang in there. I've got a better place for you."

> *"Thomas said to him, 'Lord, we don't know where You are going, so how can we know the way?'"*

---

[7] Barnes, Albert. http://www.godvine.com/bible/john/14-1. 5 Sept 2015.

In other words, "Hold on Jesus, we don't know where You are taking us. How can we trust You?" But that was precisely why they needed to trust Him. Thomas made a common mistake: he was filtering Jesus' prescription through his own human thinking. He needed to figure out where this thing was going first before he fully bought in. He wanted to know that plan before He could trust Jesus with his life.

"Daddy, I need to eat. We need to eat," my son said on one of our cross-country drives a number of years back.

"Yeah, okay, I heard you Caleb, I heard you."

Five minutes later, he insists, "Daddy, we really need to eat."

His thirteen-year-old sister Abbey said, "Well Caleb, Daddy said he heard you."

Guess what Caleb does. He sees a big billboard with a McDonald's restaurant advertisement of their yummy French fries and says out loud, "Hmmm...McDonalds, yeah!"

Seconds later, we drive past a huge golden red and yellow KFC billboard. Caleb says, "Hmmm, I love their chicken wings, Daddy!"

Caleb was unable to settle down until I stopped to eat. As we got out, Abbey said, "Caleb, when Daddy says, 'I heard you,' it means he is thinking about when to stop. He is not going to let us starve!" See, Abbey had a history with me that Caleb didn't. He wanted me to spell out the plan before he could trust me.

There Cannot Be Trust Without Uncertainty.

The answer Jesus gave to Thomas is a classic verse we have relegated to evangelism. He says, *"...I am the way, and the truth, and the life. No one comes to the Father except by Me."* (Verse 6, NKJV)

Jesus was the answer, period! And they eventually got it. Jesus became their identification. Those timid men would later love Him, even unto death.

Paul writes, *"For in Him we live, and move, and have our being..."* (Acts 17:28)

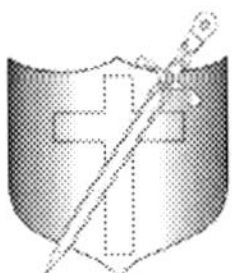

Let's read that verse again, *"Do not let your hearts be troubled. Trust in God, trust also in Me."* (John 14:1)

This scripture suggests you and I have a choice. We can control our hearts. Indeed we can tell our hearts, "Heart, do not be troubled. Trust in God."

If you will, speak to your heart right now and say, "Heart, you shall not dwell on your circumstances and freak out. Don't be afraid! You shall trust in God."

Whatever Happens, Guard Your Heart. Do Not Let It Be Troubled.

Let me conclude with Paul's promise: *"No, in all these things we are more than conquerors through Him who loved us."* (Romans 8:37)

Whether it looks like it or not, that is what we are: conquerors! We do not dwell on our changing circumstances. We trust the One who is constant, unwavering and faithful. We have a trusting faith in God.

Chapter Truths
A TRUSTING FAITH

1. Sometimes Your Experience Will Contradict Your Faith. Then What?

2. God's Primary Focus Is Not To Give To You, To Heal You, Or To Bless You. God Is Not Your Genie!

3. Your Desires Originate From Your Soul.

4. Your Desires Are Often Misguided.

5. Not All Your Desires Should Be Granted. Not All Your Prayers Should Be Answered.

6. Faith Is Incubated In The Chalice Of Ambiguity.

7. Strange That We Get Shocked When God Lovingly Withholds For Our Good; When He Acts Like God.

8. Jesus Promises Comfort—Not From Trouble, But In Spite Of It.

9. There Cannot Be Trust Without Uncertainty.

10. Whatever Happens, Guard Your Heart. Do Not Let It Be Troubled.

Chapter 15
A CERTAIN FAITH

"Be careful for nothing; but in everything by prayer and supplication with thanksgiving, let your requests be made known unto God."

Philippians 4:6

Maybe you are reading this book in an unstable part of the world. Maybe your village has been hit by some pandemic. Maybe weather patterns have changed around you so much, your crop yields have diminished and you have barely enough to feed your family, let alone a surplus to sell to others. Another commodity in rare supply today is hope. I'll tell you a little story.

An experiment was performed with two mice from the same genetic pool and with the same conditioning. They were placed in two identical barrels filled with water. The first barrel was completely covered by a dark lid. The mouse was dropped in and started to swim. It swam for about two hours until it began to sink to the bottom. The second barrel had a similar lid on it, except for a hole, just a pinprick, at the top. So, the little guy also began to swim. One hour, two hours, three hours; five, six, twelve hours; one day, two days…after three days, it was exhausted and began to sink to the bottom.

The experiment concluded the only difference between the two mice was that one had hope. The little hole in the lid allowed some light to penetrate, thus persuading the second mouse that help was coming.

Hope is important to our very existence.

A couple had just celebrated their fiftieth wedding anniversary. Sadly, it wasn't very long until the wife developed health complications and passed away. Shortly thereafter, for no apparent reason, the husband died suddenly. Psychologists attribute this phenomenon to a loss of hope. Someone I knew was misdiagnosed with cancer and given six months to live. He was told to bid his family farewell; he did, and died, almost to the day, six months later. After a few days, the physicians discovered they had made a mistake. His test results had been switched with someone else's. He had no cancer after all. But how come he died of it? His mind believed the report and somehow the cancer developed. Of course, there are lots of complicated reasons, but the culprit again was a loss of hope!

To Be Anxious
About Distress Is
To Be Human.

Says Henry D. Thoreau: "Most men live lives of quiet desperation and go to the grave with the song still in them." [8]

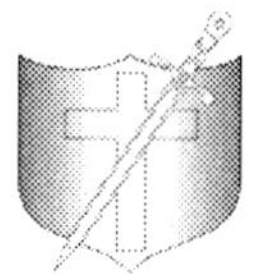

Hope is a feeling that something desirable is likely or about to happen. It is a feeling that what is wanted can actually occur.

As infants, every time we cry help comes, whether it is to feed us, change us, or simply hold us. We cry; help comes; period! Then one day we cry and help is delayed. The caretaker is either not around or feels we need to be left alone to console ourselves to sleep. That introduces some anxiety. So, we grow some more. When we cry, we are introduced to a strange notion called "*No*", and are asked to "Stop it." More anxiety ensues. One day we cry and no one comes. They no longer care to pacify us or even ask what's wrong. We are left to figure out what to do with the anxiety. We learn to distrust our own cries, and therefore our judg-

---

[8] Thoreau, Henry D. Good Reads, Inc. 2015. 5 Sept 2015
http://www.goodreads.com/quotes/search?q=lives+of+quiet+desperation

ment. Basically, every time the script is changed on us we become more anxious.

The Apostle Paul writes, *"Do not be anxious about anything..."* (Philippians 4:6a, NIV)

Now, wait there. This is coming from a guy in an uncomfortable, filthy, lower inner prison with sewage all around him. He is encouraging his free brothers and sisters to not be anxious about *anything*! Anything? Here is a fact: When you've got a situation that cannot be remedied, it's natural to be anxious. Paul is actually saying, "Guys, don't act naturally! Don't act sensibly! Don't act humanly!"

Then he adds, *"... but in every situation by prayer and petition with thanksgiving present your requests to God ..."* (Philippians 4:6b)

Our Hearts Cannot Live Without Hope. It Is The Oxygen Of The Soul.

Not just in good situations or bad situations, but in *every* situation, Paul prescribes the same antidote for worry:

Prayer, which means letting God know about it;

Petition, which involves beseeching God for His intervention;

Thanksgiving, which is a posture of surrender to His ultimate Will.

Paul adds, *"And the peace of God which transcends all understanding guard your heart and your mind in Christ Jesus."* (Philippians 4:7, NIV)

God's peace, His supernatural peace, that supersedes or transcends all understanding and logic, shall empower us to act unnaturally. If you are you sick, or losing your job and sinking into financial hardship, it is normal to be anxious. But pray, petition and give thanks, and something amazing will happen: God's peace will guard you from fear and anxiety.

Proverbs 4:23 says, *"Above all else guard your heart, for everything you do flows from it."*

The New Living Translation says, *"Guard your heart above all else, for it determines the course of your life."*

While the mind is telling you…

- You made a mistake so they are going to fire you.
- You have no money so you are stuck.
- The doctor told you this is incurable so get your house in order.
- He is going to leave you like he left his other fiancé.
- Your kids hate you so prepare to die alone.
- You cannot possibly support your family on that salary.
- The last person who did this failed, so what makes you think you are any different?

…the supernatural peace of God will transcend that negative narrative and guard your mind so you won't stay there. Therein is certain faith in God's outcome for your life.

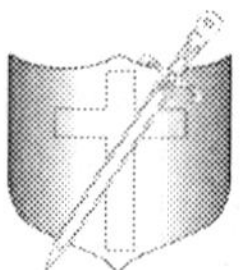

Psalms 39:7 says, *"And now, Lord, what wait I for, my hope is in Thee."*

Paul's opening words to his spiritual son, Timothy, are: *"Paul, an apostle of Jesus Christ...which is our hope."* (1 Timothy 1:1)

There can be no real hope without Christ. Jesus Christ is our true hope, my friends. Do you know Him? Do you really know Jesus Christ? If you don't, or if you feel unsure, I tell you once again what Peter said to that jailor: *"Believe on the Lord Jesus Christ, and you will be saved, you and your household."* (Acts 16:31, NIV)

That's it! No need for scripted prayers. Simply believe in Jesus with all your heart and you are on your way!

As I close this book, let me share Paul's prayer to the Romans:

> *"May the God of hope fill you with all joy and peace as you trust in Him so that you may overflow with hope by the power of the Holy Spirit."*(Romans 15:13, NIV)

The Peace Of God Is The Guardian Of Your Mind. Without It, Anxiety Is Inevitable!

Nineteenth Century businessman-turned-pastor Edward Mote wrote a song, which became an old-time favorite. I sing it every so often:

My hope is built on nothing less
Than Jesus' blood and righteousness;
I dare not trust the sweetest frame,
But wholly lean on Jesus' name.

On Christ the solid Rock I stand;
All other ground is sinking sand,
All other ground is sinking sand.

When darkness veils His lovely face,
I rest on His unchanging grace;
In every high and stormy gale,
My anchor holds within the veil.

His oath, His covenant, His blood
Support me in the whelming flood;
When all around my soul gives way
He then is all my hope and stay.

When He shall come with trumpet sound,
Oh, may I then in Him be found;
Dressed in His righteousness alone,
Faultless to stand before the throne.

On Christ, the solid Rock, I stand;
All other ground is sinking sand.
All other ground is sinking sand.[9]

---

[9] Mote, Edward. *"My Hope is Built on Nothing Less."* Harry Plantinga. 2007-present. http://www.hymnary.org/text/my_hope_is_built_on_nothing_less. 5 Sept. 2015

Chapter Truths
A CERTAIN FAITH

1. **Our Hearts Cannot Live Without Hope. It Is The Oxygen Of The Soul.**

2. **To Be Anxious About Distress Is To Be Human.**

3. **The Peace Of God Is The Guardian Of Your Mind. Without It, Anxiety Is Inevitable!**

Chapter 16
A SELFLESS FAITH

"...Surely this is the Prophet who is to come into the world."

John 6:14 (NIV)

Let me tell you a story conveyed by all the gospel writers. It is one of Jesus' most famous miracles. Allow me to share it from the perspective of the main character: the young lad.

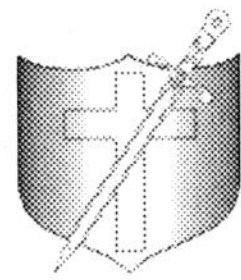

Life is hard; the economy is depressed. We are Israelites, subjects of the cruel Roman Empire. Oh, they are brutal. They are vicious. So, most of us are angry, bitter and constantly anxious about our overall well-being.

I have to work really hard and have had to since I was a boy. I sell barley for extra revenue for our close-knit, hard-working family. Nothing ever comes easy for us, even life itself. Death seems commonplace with all the constant insurrections and uprisings. I do not see an end to this occupation. It makes me wonder if I will ever grow up, become a man someday, and have a family. Hopelessness; yes that is my daily estate—sheer hopelessness! Although, some among us still believe God has not forgotten about us, His special people.

The past few months have been different for us. First, there was this man named John. They called him a prophet, the first real prophet in nearly four hundred years. His miraculous birth was said to have been foretold by an angel. He liked to hang out in the back wilderness and the harsh desert places. He was old-school alright— rough clothing made of camel hair and a strange diet of locusts and wild honey. But, his simple message moved multitudes: “Prepare the way of the Lord. Make straight paths for Him!”

Of course, nobody really understood what he meant, but, boy, did he ever speak with conviction! He spoke of the coming of the *ONE*. He said his mission was to, *“... turn the hearts of the fathers to the children, and the disobedient to the wisdom of the just; to make ready a people prepared for the Lord.”* (Luke 1:17)

Many got converted and were baptized. Was he the Messiah? We hoped he was; we so wanted him to be. Though there were those who claimed to be, none had made such an impact and turned the hearts of so many. So, we pressed him for an answer. “No, I am not He ... I am just the voice of one crying in the wilderness.”

John would speak out against Herod and was arrested; hope dashed yet again.

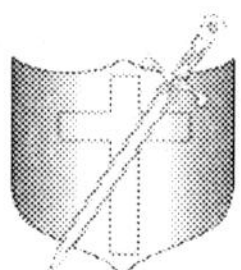

Well, these days everybody is talking about John’s cousin Jesus. Yeah! Evidently, John himself said Jesus was the Lamb of God. Is this the Son of David, the long-awaited Messiah? Could it be true? We all know what happened to the others who falsely claimed the title: they were crucified!

But Jesus...He seems different. They talk about His brilliance, His miracles. They talk about how He heals the blind, the deaf, and delivers demoniacs from oppression with a single command. He even cleanses lepers. Yes, lepers! Those diseased outcasts who are isolated in colonies outside the city walls. No illness or condition seems too big for Jesus. Some even say He raises the dead.

He gathers mammoth crowds, but, unlike John, He actually walks up and down through our cities, and even goes to our synagogues. He is fearless, confronting our rulers about their hypocrisy. Everyone here wants to hear Him and see Him. Everyone wants to touch Him or be touched by Him. Jesus of Nazareth has come to bring us hope.

Today, I am going to go see Him. I can't wait!

It will be Passover soon, so crowds are going to be really thick with people coming from all over to celebrate the feast. I am told Jesus is hanging out on the mountainside today. So, I gotta make my way out early enough. In fact, I'm not going to have lunch. I will just grab some leftover barley and a couple of fish. I'll eat after I get there and get settled.

So, I head out and yeah this is actually much bigger than was rumored, indeed much bigger than I thought. There are all kinds of people heading out to the mountainside: I see cripples on mats, and blind people being guided up the mountain. I see the destitute, along with the rich. I think I even see some lepers in the distance, trying to remain inconspicuous. Wait—I also see Roman soldiers heading out to see this Jewish Rabbi. The anticipation is beyond anything I have ever experienced.

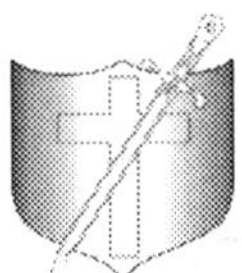

Finally we are there. I have got to make my way to the front; don't want to miss anything. Being agile, I squeeze through to the very front section of the vast crowd.

Oh, I see Him, I see Jesus. He is a little taller than I thought, actually. Oh, but He is everything they said and more. His words, His compassion, His wisdom, His grace, and His very countenance—all simply enthralling! I have never felt like this before.

My heart is racing; I am captivated by Jesus. Time seems to fly by until my tummy grumbles—I am hungry; everyone here must be. The kids have started crying. It's about lunchtime, you know, but what's the plan? Will Jesus stop the meeting and dismiss us to go find something to eat? It is remote here; no towns or markets anywhere close by. Glad I packed something.

Jesus notices. It's like He hears my thoughts. His compassion-filled eyes scan the crowd. I see Him talking to one of His disciples, Phillip. We know Phillip. He is from Bethesda, and if anyone can come up with a workable solution, it would be this homeboy. But what can they really do? I know this ministry is big, but surely they can't feed us all! There's got to be at least five thousand men here. And with the women and kids, easily eight thousand people.

Suddenly I hear a voice, "Hey son, what's that?"

It's Andrew, one of His other disciples.

"It's my lunch," I reply. "Nothing much, just five loaves of bread and two fish!"

"Well, give it to me," he commands.

Before I have time to think, I hand him my box. Next thing I know, we are all being asked to sit down in groups. Yes, Jesus has instructed us all to sit back down. I am watching with much intrigue as Andrew gives Jesus my lunch. Is He going to eat it? Well? To my pleasant surprise, Jesus opens it up, lifts it up to the heavens and He gives thanks.

We are all transfixed and curious. I am excited. My lunch is in Jesus' hands. Something is happening here; something really special and powerful. Jesus does not take long. He hands my lunch to His disciples and He motions them to distribute to us. So, I am thinking: is He asking them to give the pieces to the feeblest among us? What could this small meal possibly do? And why? Why would He even do this?

And right away, they begin to pass it around.

Wait. Where did that basket come from? And that one? Oh, and that one over there? There are baskets full of bread and fish everywhere. What?

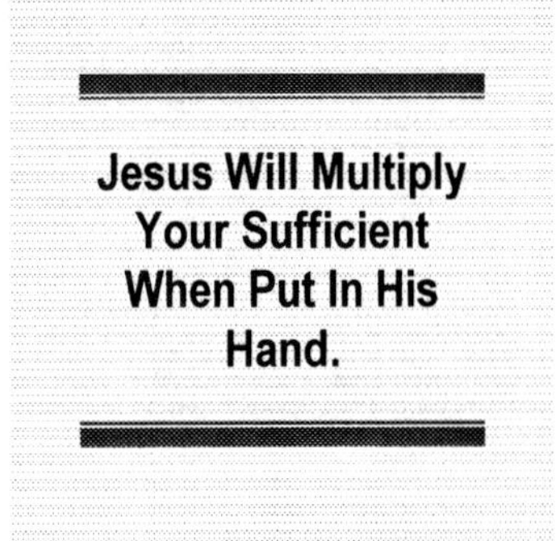

Jesus Will Multiply
Your Sufficient
When Put In His
Hand.

The screams and laughter: "Food! So much food!" Fish and bread, more fish, more bread—everywhere! It's a miracle! How could He do that to my little lunch? Well, we are all hungry, so we don't really think too much except to take and eat. And we eat and eat until we are so full. We are giggling with euphoria; it's just incredible. There is so much food that He tells the disciples to actually gather leftovers. Leftovers? Thousands fed miraculously, not just enough, but so much so that there are leftovers: twelve full baskets! My mother would never believe what happened today.

Awe fills the mountainside. We begin to murmur and whisper, to worship Jesus saying:

"Surely this is the Prophet who is to come into the world." (John 6:14)

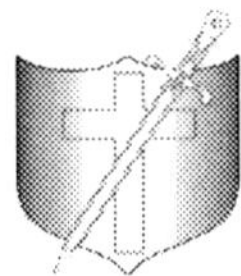

I ask you, my friends, where is your lunch? Where do you keep your reserves? Do you have a lunch box stashed away for that rainy day? Where is your stash; your proverbial parachute?

- Is it your savings account? You never know when things might go awry, right? At least you have some money set aside for that rainy day.

- Is it your retirement package? At least your later days shall be bountiful with endless cruises and golfing excursions.

- Is it your health? Thank God for those genes, right?

- Is it your pedigree? Perhaps your family history, connections or social network ensures you will always have a way around anything in your local community.

- Is it your wealth? Do you come from a rich or a developed country? A brother once told me, "Hey I am from Sweden, I may not have much but my country will always take care of me."

What is your lunch? Jesus wants it all. He is asking for your lunch today. He can do way more with it than you ever can. His desire goes beyond your sustenance. Jesus wants to take the little you have; to bless the little you have, and to feed multitudes with it. He wants to prepare a feast of Faith from your meager provisions.

God Uses Our Adequate To Feed Multitudes.

I speak with such conviction, friends, because I've lived this. I should be dead, or at best completely lost in the little village in Mukono, in the East African nation of Uganda where I was born. I shouldn't have such a blessed life. I shouldn't have such a beautiful wife as Ingrid. How does a Ugandan musician connect so miraculously with a Romanian student in Chicago, USA? Only by God's grace. We shouldn't have such an amazing family: our boys Adam, Celeb, Judah, and Elijah, along with our princess, Abbey. Remember, with a life expectancy of thirty-seven where I was born, I was never supposed to grow up, much less do anything big with my life.

I shouldn't have this incredible ministry that is touching hundreds of millions around the world today. I do not belong on these stages, but rather in my remote Ugandan village. I shouldn't have these fine friends, this incredible health or this wonderful education. Oh, but the Grace of God!

Some think it has to be some kind of super talent. Others say I am a master strategist, maybe an ardent fundraiser, or an expert campaigner.

Some imagine I must have a network of influential connections, big money promoters or deep-pocketed partners. I assure you, it is none of those things.

I am not a best-selling author, a politician or a relationship connoisseur. I don't sleep enough, eat right, or exercise regularly. What I have is a simple, yet very precious history. Decades ago, I took my five loaves and two fishes and gave them to Jesus. He took whatever I had—my voice, talent, skills, personality, relationships, and my very essence. Jesus touched my measly lunch, blessed it, multiplied it and now feeds the world with it.

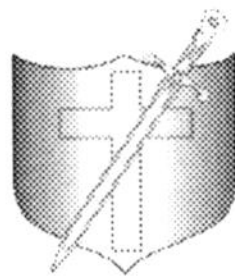

Here is the most exciting truth: what God did for me, He can also do for you—and much more. He is doing it all over the world. The Apostle Peter declares in the book of Acts:

> *"...Of a truth I perceive that God is no respecter of persons."* (Acts 10:34)

The New International version says, *"God shows no favoritism."*

The New Living Translation says, *"God plays no favorites."*

I think that is amazing. God extends the same favor to the Ethiopian as He does to the Swede, the Russian or the Korean. To each of us, He asks, "Will you give Me your lunch; your everything?"

Jesus said,

> *"Whoever wants to save his life will lose it, but whosoever loses his life for My sake will save it."* (Luke 9:24, NKJV)

Let me close this book with this challenge:

What do you have in your hand? What is it that you think you own? Give it to Jesus! Give Him your savings, your connections, your job, your wealth, your net worth, your wife, your husband, your kids, your security, your pedigree, your comforts—your everything! Let Him bless it, multiply it, and feed your neighbors, your village, your city, your country and the whole world.

God Is More Interested In Your Availability Than Your Ability.

Chapter Truths
A SELFLESS FAITH

1. **Jesus Will Multiply Your Sufficient When Put In His Hand.**

2. **God Uses Our Adequate To Feed Multitudes.**

3. **God Plays No Favorites!**

4. **God Is More Interested In Your Availability Than Your Ability.**

CLOSING THOUGHT

There it is. What do you think? More crucially, did it stir you? Or did it merely stimulate you intellectually or provoke you theologically? God forbid! It would be beneficial for you to read it again and again.

Paul writes, *"Above all, taking the shield of faith, wherewith ye shall be able to quench all the fiery darts of the wicked."* (Ephesians 6:16)

The Greek word for “shield” there is the word *thureos*. It means a wide, oblong, four-cornered door. A Roman shield completely covered the Roman soldier. *The thureos* was composed of multiple layers of tightly woven animal hide. It was thick, durable and as strong as steel. It was by far the most important piece of armor in any soldier's arsenal.

But there was one vitally important thing every Roman soldier had to do: they had to *maintain* their shields. Each soldier was given a vial of oil. Every morning, they would rub the heavy ointment into the leather portion of the shield to keep it soft and pliable. Failure to do this would render the shield stiff and ineffective. A poorly maintained shield would easily crack and fall apart. Neglect the daily application of oil and invite certain death! Every Roman soldier knew it!

Paul is deliberate in using this imagery in describing the importance of faith. Faith is critical to the believer's life. Without it, we are defenseless. In my missionary travels around the world, countless people have said:

> *"Dr. Dennis, I used to have faith. No matter what the enemy threw at me, I was immovable! Well, these days, anything and everything seems to shake me. I entertain the wildest fears. I wonder what happened?"*

It's simple: they didn't oil their shields. Oil signifies the Holy Spirit. Without a daily fresh touch of the Spirit of God, your faith becomes hard, stiff, and brittle. One little dart from the enemy and a poorly maintained shield crumbles.

So, a final word of encouragement I leave with you: Maintain your shield. Maintain your faith. Just because you had faith yesterday doesn't mean you are all set for the rest of your days. Just because you believed God through your last victory, doesn't mean you are prepared for your next giant! Maintain–Maintain–Maintain.

Godspeed on your journey!

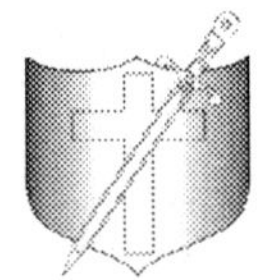

"NOW FAITH IS THE ASSURANCE (THE CONFIRMATION, THE TITLE DEED) OF THE THINGS [WE] HOPE FOR, BEING THE PROOF OF THINGS [WE] DO NOT SEE AND THE CONVICTION OF THEIR REALITY [FAITH PERCEIVING AS REAL FACT WHAT IS NOT REVEALED TO THE SENSES]."

HEBREWS 11:1 (AMP)

ABOUT DENNIS

Dennis was born in the small town of Mukono, in the African nation of Uganda. On December 12, 1980, he accepted Jesus Christ into his life, and was immediately called to full-time ministry. In 1987, he co-founded the award-winning *Limit X*, a trio which would become one of Africa's most successful gospel music outfits.

In 2004, he co-founded the *International College of Excellence* in Chicago, which quickly grew to twenty-two extension campuses in multiple countries. In 2007, he founded *Eagle's Wings International*, a global missionary organization, and planted *Sanctuary of Life Church* the following year.

In 2009, he launched *Eagle's Wings Bible Institute* in Chicago where he still serves as academic Dean and Chancellor.

Dennis holds two master's degrees and three doctorate degrees, and has authored over a dozen books. As a Global Peace Ambassador, he is a highly sought-after speaker who also serves on numerous boards of corporations around the world. He has served Jesus Christ as a missionary in seventy countries on five continents.

Dennis has been married to Ingrid, his beloved wife, for twenty years. God has blessed them with five precious children: Adam, Abigail, Caleb, Judah and Elijah. They reside in the great state of Texas, USA.

Contact information:

Dr. Dennis D. Sempebwa
President & Founder,
Eagle's Wings International
Website: www.e-wings.net
Facebook: facebook.com/dennis.d.sempebwa
Twitter: @dsempebwa